Deuxième Folie

Susan Marloye-James

Painted by Alfred B...
Braine-le-Comte

Print information available on the last page.

Rev. date: 06/29/2019

To order additional copies of this book, contact:
Xlibris
0800-056-3182
www.xlibrispublishing.co.uk
Orders@ Xlibrispublishing.co.uk

This book is dedicated to my

First Mate

who is also my husband, the other Folie

and love of my life

First Mate

PROLOGUE

The question always is why a boat? The answer of course is we got the 'bug' about navigating on waterways and ended up building our own boat to explore some of Europe's densely covered waterways.

The United Kingdom is extremely rich in waterways, either natural resources or canals built for commercial purposes; thus, the so-called "narrow boats" where the initial resources to transport non-time dependent goods around at low cost. Where road and railways starting competing with the waterways, the narrow boats became attractive for individuals' pleasure 'caravanning' on areas with dense waterway systems. Having always been attracted by the water, we decided that some navigation on the British waterways would tell us if we liked this kind of 'relaxation'. Therefore, we decided on a trial cruise on the Avon, we rented a narrow boat at Upton Marina on the Severn.

After a short navigation with an instructor to learn how to handle the boat (less than 30 minutes), back to the Marina where the teacher jumped off and pushed us in the middle of the stream. To join the Avon we had to navigate the Avon lock and face a smiling lock keeper: "Don't worry I am used to beginners" – very encouraging! Therefore, off we were on our way to Stratford our goal and we learned a lot during this first experience: passing through locks with and most without lock keepers, control of the speed backwards and forwards, friendly help from other boating people and bystanders, especially for mooring near to pubs and of course pub grub. Altogether, we were successful in not sinking the boat and handed it back without being penalized for any damage!

The cruising bug was definitely instilled in our blood now and the next learning trip was to take on the French waterways hiring from the Blue Line if memory serves us correct from Auxerre with the intention of trying the Canal de Bóurgogne. Unfortunately, the water level was too low on that Canal so we cruised l'Yonne, as we had only one week, due to work commitments; we made the most of it. The highlight of the trip was mooring up on Quai d'Épizy at Joigny and booking into Jean-Michael Lorain's Michelin 3* 'La Côte Saint Jacques' for a gourmet evening. The memory lingers on, especially when they arrived with the cheeses, there must have been over 50 laid out, not wanting to look stupid Sue asked for Brie, only to be told 'it was out of season' – still not sure about that reply, did they just not have any?

Another trip with Blue Line starting from their base on the Canal du Midi. On the way down, we stopped off at Cahors visit a retired friend Marcel Doyen. This trip towards Marseillan (Sue's first oysters) heading back rapidly due to the heavy rain and rising water, made it in time for the round lock in Adge before it closed and onto the Canal du Midi. Then on to Beziers and its flight of locks, extremely impressive, especially going upstream and the lock keeper opens two in one go to speed things up! we would do it again with our boat eventually. We learnt a lot more on this trip and little did we know at that time we would end up living in Ségala for our first retirement.

One last trip took place on the Thames, starting at Shepperton, the narrow boat was looking dilapidated from the outside but all the mechanical parts were nearly new. The rental agent started with us for the customary training but after the first lock, he simply said: "why did I bother, have a good trip". Awaiting entry to a lock, the dilapidated boat, which led a snobby crew of a 'posh' cruiser to make some stupid comments, resulted in us switching speak French. They then decided to try to speak pigeon French to us but Sue in her best British accent said "actually dear chaps I speak English", no more problems. Worth mentioning, it was during this trip that we could moor nearby and see the Magna Carta Memorial at Runnymede and we took out a small licence to cruise down the Wey and into Guildford. This was to be our last trip with hired boats as Deuxième Folie was nearing completion and our money had to go towards that, especially as the hiring costs had augmented over the years.

LA FOLIE

Although we were definitely infected with the bug for waterway cruising, we had to 'suspend' our desire for this kind of relaxation when we bought a dilapidated house in 1983. Sue (The Captain) had by that time moved and joined the SHAPE Headquarters in Mons and Jacques (The First Mate) was still at the NATO Programming Centre near Liege and we were together once a week under the roof of Jacques' mother's home in Andenne. Buying this property would enable us to be together in reasonable distance from Liege via the motorways. Financial restraints meant that we could only order repairs above our bricolage capabilities e.g. a new roof, insert a chimney and fireplace. Sue in the meantime had been sleeping on a mattress on the floor with a working bathroom and kitchen (after the latter had been cleaned).

In 1985, Jacques finally managed to join NATO in Brussels and thus more hours would be available to the continuing restoration of the old farmhouse and join Sue on the mattress. After five years we could say "whatever is left to do is not urgent and of minor importance". LA FOLIE was there.

DEUXIEME FOLIE

At that point, we looking at the amount and diversity of the tools we had amassed after the works on La Folie, we decided that they should not be unemployed and would help us in fulfilling our dream: build a canal boat.

The First Mate had met an owner of a small boat on the water expanse at Vilvorde who had met an 'old' man François Conscience. He had a friend who was building fiberglass boats both because he enjoyed it and it was his source of revenue. We met him, he had just completed a small sightseeing boat destined to navigate on a small touristic lake in the Ardennes, and the mould had not been discarded and was thus available to use if anyone could come with an order in the near future. The design was far from what we would have liked but we could easily convince the builder to alter the design to fit our view, since what we were asking for did not require changes to the mould. When the boat shell was finished and the mould removed, we were granted access to it to complete the work, i.e. add the mechanical parts that would make it a navigable entity. François was more than happy to help us and he installed the main propulsion system and related controls. Our experience cruising led us to believe we needed a bow prop and François agreed to do that job, thus demonstrating he too was a specialist in 'fiber glazing'. We were able to afford the cost of the technical parts thanks to Sue's privileges of tax-free purchases enjoyed by foreign members of SHAPE.

When ready to join the water the boat shell was removed using a heavy-duty mobile crane. The 'skeleton' was lowered and the propeller went into the water and to our 'horror' (including François), water started pouring into the bilge. François and his son Roger who was helping him rushed to the nearest supermarket to buy bricks and fast drying cement with an additive. After their efforts, things went smoothly and 'Deuxième Folie' was launched with a bottle of champagne and was happily floating on the water ready to move. We moved it initially stopping on the way at the Brussels Royal Yacht Club (BRYC) of which we were members who could enjoy the facilities, one or two people looked the other way when they saw what was moored up. Thanks to Sue's nationality, Deuxième Folie had been registered in Jersey and was legally allowed in all waters and we were already enjoying our navigation permits, which we achieved through SHAPE contacts after a very elementary examination. Thus, Deuxième Folie was born out of a mould for a Bateau Mouche, sadly that mould ended up in a rubbish dump meaning she could never be replicated.

We had prior to this time met Bruno Urbain and his family who owned a restaurant (Belle Vue) in Ronquières and through one of many stops there for liquid we met Charlie who worked for Belgian Canal Services. Thanks to him, we managed to obtain a mooring on the Old Samme Branch of Ronquières to the Petite Bouffe, which gave us an easy place to work on the boat. It also required installation of electricity, the small house nearby gave us permission to put the box on their wall. That was the easy bit because we had to burrow under the towpath in order to safely install the main cable and make sure it was correctly earthed. This we did and it was duly inspected and passed.

May this book inspire all those who have folly ideas, to follow them through even though the word 'folie' can also be understood as absurd, inane, madness, it is and it is not but the sense of achievement and satisfaction far outweighs any derogatory remarks

<u>PHOTOS OF THE LAUNCHING</u>

Photos of Launch

WORK IN PROGRESS PHOTOS

Works on the Interior

CHAPTER ONE - FIRST VOYAGE

30th April – 24th May 1991

Before starting, we should make it clear Sue was the Captain, being an ex-Wren she has to take priority over Jacques who was allocated the rank of First Mate; well he only had Belgian Air Force in his CV.

30th April. Today we were determined to start our adventures with Deuxième Folie, who was still in an unfinished state, with no door at that point just tarpaulin. We left our permanent mooring via the two small locks off the old Samme Branch of Ronquières to the Petite Bouffe by 15:00 hours obviously late to bed due to Eric and the doors, he returned at 06:00 hours on the 1st May and we finally had doors, although not fitting brilliantly.

2nd May. We finally left at 12:30 hours and waited to enter the Ronquières Inclined Plane (Plan Incliné), which is a Belgian canal inclined plane on the Brussels-Charleroi Canal in the province of Hainaut in Wallonia that opened in April 1968 after a six-year construction period and it is this that replaced the old Samme River mentioned above. It is located in the municipality of Braine-le-Comte, where we live and takes its name from the nearby village of Ronquières and we finally ascended at 15:00 hours very impressive, very high to walk around to the office with see-through floor in order to get our necessary stamp on documentation!

Ronquières

We continued on to the next three seven metre locks, first one (Viesville) no problem but the second (Gosseliers) BIG PROBLEM, steam pouring out of the galley – hot water pipes had blown, water inside as well as outside. Third lock (Marchienne-au-Pont) engine died and Jacques (The First Mate) had to pull the Captain and her boat out. Got it going again and moored up at 19:30 hours at Marchienne-au-Pont. Phoned Ian (Sue's son) he and Melissa found us in record time took all the soggy towels home and brought replacement ones and the bicycle plates, required by law, (we actually could ride bikes at that time). Even with the problems, we had still managed to make forty-two kilometres and four locks!

3rd May. The overnight stop was OK but no water. Got up early and went shopping for 'copper piping' as it was the reinforced plastic that burst! Plenty of Brico shops around and we made the necessary purchases. Jacques worked all morning replacing the hot water piping and it was finally working. We tanked up with 150 litres of water moved onto La Sambre and reached the first lock of the day at 14:30 hours the weather was still awful we even had hail!

The locks are much smaller on the Sambre, which is a left-bank tributary of the Meuse, but the whole area was much prettier. We managed to lock through nine of the ten locks before the frontier, just making the ninth at 19:15 hours Moored up in the countryside, very peaceful a long hard day and another 30 kilometres clocked up and the nine locks, Landelies, Abbaye d'Aulne, Trou d'Aulne, Grand Courant, Thuin, Lobbes, Fontaine Valmont, La Buissière and Solre sur Sambre.

4th May. Left at 08:50 hours and arrived at the last lock (Erquelinnes de Monceau) at 09:15 hours, took the last paper and arrived at the Belgian customs at 09:30 hours and left at 09:50 hours pretty good going even though it was not without difficulties. French customs easy. We bought our first baguette at Jeumont. As the day progressed the weather deteriorated, rain, rain, rain. The doors leaked but we finally made it to Landrecies a little village in the North of France where La Sambre became the Canal de la Sambre à l'Oise having had to follow two barges who just fitted into the locks. Here we had a town mooring with 220V available and a distance of 60 kilometres covered and twelve locks (including Maubeuge, Hautmont, and Berlaimont just to mention a few).

5th May. Locks not working as it was Sunday so we had a very busy day doing carpentry and running repairs. The sun came out but by the end of the afternoon, our friend the rain was back. Met the crew of BENTHA, another British ship, they had spent seven months in Belgium and were off to France for the allotted six months. I should mention here that running repairs continued throughout the trip, even during lunch breaks we would stop, put the generator on, and work!

6th May. Left at 07:00 hours to face a day with twenty-seven locks seven of which were automated but the 'moped gang' followed us. In addition to the locks, we clocked up another 43 kilometres. We stopped at Origny-Ste-Benoît intending to shop but it was an industrial town and we moved just out of town to moor for the night. A lovely quiet evening but during the night the alarm clock fell and we had to hide it under the duvet to stop the noise.

7th May. Entered another series of automated locks at 07:50 hours (only ten this time) and we had our next problem on entering the second lock, no instruments only the rudder working, no log or depth and worst of all no bow prop. Brilliant steering by the Captain got us all the way to Compiegne on the Oise River of WW1 history, in a small marina with all facilities where we just fitted in. It was a long day covering some sixty-eight kilometres and fourteen locks.

8th May. Morning was spent doing odd jobs, Sue did the shopping, and Jacques ended up in the water trying to solve the bow prop problem. It remains unsolved, but suspicions rest on a burnt out motor.

We continued on our way covering sixty-two kilometres but only five locks, the good news was that we were only using 3.6 litres of fuel instead of ten which the book said. Having passed industrial areas, forests, Port Salut, the Pont de St. Maxence and Verneuil-en-Halatte, Creil – again industrial, Précy-sur-Oise, Boran-sur-Oise, we ended mooring up that evening at Beaumont-sur-Oise an old fortified market town built on the high ground on the banks of the Oise.

9th May. We left around 09:00 hours continuing on l'Oise for thirty-five kilometres and two locks to join the Seine, passing l'Isle-Adam, Pontoise and Conflans-Ste-Honorine. Because moorings were, few and far between we continued for another forty-two kilometres, crazy in hindsight but only one lock (écluse de Bougival). We passed under many bridges interestingly one name Pont rails des Anglais, also a large Port (Genneviliers) with it six quays and St. Denis eventually mooring up at Port Sisley at Villeneuve-la-Garenne, guarded moorings at a price of 130FF per night.

Entry into Paris on the Seine

10th May. Leaving at 10:30 hours we were enroute for Paris passing one lock (écluse de Suresnes) and then 30 kilometres unbelievably in the sun. This was something the Captain had been looking forward to entering Paris via the Seine it was wonderful, passing the sightseeing boats, lovers on the side everything you expect to see. There were very comprehensive instructions on how to move on this part of the Seine who had priority, small boats, sightseeing, etc. and which arch to pass under the bridges, of which there were many. We moored up at the Port de plaisance de Paris-Arsenal which is just below Place de la Bastille. Seeing the 'Red Duster' several came out to help, they did not stay long when seeing the state of our boat! One and a half hours after mooring our friend the rain was back again. At least we had all mod cons here and would not leave until 13th May. We obviously worked on the boat; the First Mate was a little naughty as whilst painting (with blue paint) it splashed on a rather posh white boat next to us. He hopped over and tried to clean it and luckily we could move our boat to another mooring inside and no one was any the wiser (that we were aware of!). We visited some favourite sights, Montmartre of course and Sue managed not to buy another painting and ate out obviously with the Bastille area nearby we had plenty of choices.

13th May. Left the port at 09:00 hours, headed out of Paris, and joined the Marne, which was only five kilometres away. At the first lock (St. Maurice), we lost one and a half hours and at the second (St. Maur) forty-five minutes not a good start. However, things improved and the scenery was lovely as well as the weather. We went through two tunnels, the first called St. Maur and the second was between two locks (Chalifert and Lesches) and unnamed. We had overall an adventurous day ending when we moored up at 19:15 hours at a charming little harbour in Poincy, lovely spot. Fantastic restaurant an l'ancien moulin (Hostellerie du Moulin), this was our once a trip gourmet meal, intended to keep the menu but that has been lost over the years.

14th May. Left after a peaceful night at 09:15 hours we had again a long day eighty-eight kilometres and seven locks. Lovely scenery not a lot of commercial traffic, First Mate had a bad burn from the ropes on one finger, blamed the Captain. Some lovely names on the way, St-Jean-les-deux Jumeaux, La Ferte-sous-Jouarre, Méry-sur-Marne and Chateau-Thierry, to mention a few. Moored up at 19:15 hours at Jaulgonne, still on the Marne very peaceful and had all facilities thus just made Alimentation! urgent need for WINE.

15th May. Well another eventful day. Left at 08:20 hours and everything was fine we had croissants for breakfast. We made four locks (Vandières, Damery, Cumière, Dizy) the first three were sloping, first with big pillars, the last two of these we locked through with a barge. After the last lock, we turned on to the Canal latéral à la Marne. We were all set to enter our first automatic (i.e. with perch) Epernay – calamity. The flexible coupling of the shaft separated itself from the gearbox – i.e. no brakes; luckily, we headed for the trees. One and a half hours later after fishing in the bilge for bolts and gaskets, the First Mate mended it, we were off, and another five locks to Conde. We turned into the junction Canal de l'Aisne a la Marne, we started the ladder of eight automatic locks (Conde, Coupé, Isse, Fosse, St. Martin & Longues-Raies) and were locked in at 19:30 hours between the 6th and 7th (Longues-Raies & Champ-bon-Garçon). We moored up – no other choice – in the middle of country thinking of 06:30 hours start having covered sixty-two kilometres and fifteen locks.

16th May. So playing it by the rules we were up engine running and ready at 06:30 hours sure enough one came through we moved in after him at 06:40 hours therefore, the day started with the remaining Champ-bon-Garçon and Vandemange locks. We then went through our longest tunnel yet Mont-de-Billy two and a half kilometres, quite something, we then continued as far as Reims where we shopped and refueled (125 ltrs.). End of the afternoon we picked up a bit of commercial traffic so did not make the last lock, so once again we were locked in and stuck with another 06:30 hours start!! Beautiful evening weather wise after a cold wet morning. We had covered fifty-two kilometres, eighteen locks and one 2,302-metre tunnel and ended up nearby Berry-au-Bac.

17ᵗʰ May. As anticipated early start at 06:30 hours and the lights turned green and off we were through the lock we did make yesterday, then we were soon turning into the Canal latéral à l'Aisne, which eventually changed into the Canal des Ardennes. Freezing cold, a layer of ice on the boat and the mists rising off the water. It warmed up a little but still needed jumpers and the doors stayed shut all day. Good day none the less and we passed twelve locks, not wanting to name them all just a few interesting names: Fléchambault, Courcy, Loivre, and Moulin de Sapigneul. We only had two problems one where the radar did not work and we had to ring for assistance and one where the doors did not shut properly so we were half way up and had to stop and empty it again and then refill. All these locks had been activate by a 'perch' a hanging pole with a twisting mechanism at the bottom, so you had to move slowly up to it, missed a couple of times but then got used to the manoeuvre. Moored up at 16:30 hours in a nice little village called Attigny, which had a good routier (transport café) could have been La Truite Au Bleu where we had a four-course meal for 50FF for two.

18ᵗʰ May. Well the third early start 06:40 hours was, however, short lived, as the mist rising from the water was so bad we could not see, so it was some forty-five minutes later that we entered the first lock the day. After the second we geared ourselves up for the twenty-six automated locks of the Vallée de Montgon that lay ahead and the book informed us it would take seven hours. The First Mate had made a makeshift pole to knock the radar beam, only missed three then my lovely Mate got a system to recover but it took nearly one hour for the first three. Then the Engineer alias my lovely First Mate telephoned from the control box and following the instructions given and we were off again. We then started to progress really well, lost and recovered a fender and got stuck in some mud otherwise fine until entering the third lock from the end, the shaft disconnected again – i.e. no brakes – threw the ropes to my First Mate and for once I did not miss thus we did not crash. The hard working First Mate then pulled us out of the lock manually, well the Captain had to steer didn't she! Back to searching in the bilge again, but horrors on finding it the thread had gone. The Captain had to get active this time, got the bike off the boat and she set off for the village of Le Chesne, found a garage and acquired the necessary bits some five kilometre round trip. First Mate repaired us and after one and a half hours pushed us away from the bank in triumph and fell in, actually, he tried to jump on board and missed. We finally made the last two locks entered Le Chesne and moored at 16:30 hours the day was finally over having covered a mere sixteen kilometres and an incredible twenty-eight lock thank goodness it is Sunday tomorrow and a lie-in as it is Pentecost (Whitsun) so no locks working. So just relaxing but working on the boat as usual.

20th May. Refreshed from our semi-quiet day we set off at 07:45 hours in drizzle, which eventually stopped. Passed a couple of barges going upstream in fact all peace and quiet until we reached the turn to enter the tunnel of St. Aignan which was one way only and you needed your lights and ended up on a mud bank stranded! not marked on the maps. Therefore, Tarzan, alias First Mate, had to get to work. We took down the dinghy joined two long ropes together and then he rowed to the other side. After several false attempts and sheer brute force, he pulled us off and collapsed in a big heap for once not in the water, but as he was wet from the knees down from the dinghy – change of clothes again. We made the tunnel and went straight into the lock. The lock keeper knew about the mud and agreed that perhaps some warning should have been put!! Glad to say the rest of the day passed without further disasters. At Pont-à- Bar we turned into the Meuse and we knew then that we were unfortunately heading home. We moored up at Monthermé in the placement of the bateau mouche at the owner's invitation. That day we covered sixty-five kilometres, thirteen locks and of course that one tunnel with the muddy approach.

First Mate extracting us from the mud

21st May. We actually had a day without rain and saw some beautiful scenery, loads of Dutch barges on the go. We covered sixty kilometres, sixteen locks just to mention one No. 48 écluse des Dames de Meuse; it was here that the unfaithful wives Hodieme, Berthe and Iges were turned into stone by divine wrath! in addition, two tunnels one not on the map and the other was literally carved through the rocks, unfortunately unnamed on the map.

One incident a barge rammed us because he thought we were too slow leaving a lock! the Captain stood up to it! The lock keeper was not amused and informed us that the bargee would find the next locks closed to him for the minimum waiting time of twenty minutes, felt better after hearing that. The important event of the day was crossing back into Belgium after Givet and coping with the Belgian Customs and we were now in possession of the famous B5 form and are legally in transit in Belgium. We moored up at Hastière and dined on the B5.

22nd May. First Mate completed a vidange prior to start, filter had to be rinsed in petrol and we could not get a new one. Lovely day on the Meuse, beautiful scenery passing through Dinant a major tourist centre with slated roofed houses lining up on both sides of the Meuse, Wepion we passed unbelievable houses, the Belgian equivalent of the Thames would be a good example. Total day was sixty-two kilometres, twelve locks and final resting place was Andenne having passed Namur, ready for tomorrow mornings pick-up. Filled up with 172 litres of Diesel.

23rd May. Marraine (Jacques' Mum) arrived at 07:15 hours with breakfast and we moved off at 07:45 hours Marraine riding with us back to Namur. Weather nice but cold. The first lock, the large one at Andenne was full with us roped to a 76-metre tanker! Poor Marraine was in total panic and rushed to the loo. After dropping off Marraine in Namur (do not think she will try the experience again) we then turned into the Sambre and the day passed uneventfully but did not make the last lock (Viesville) as intended. Total trip that day was seventy-three kilometres and nine locks.

24th May. Left the outskirts of Charleroi and headed home we were really coming to the end of our first trip. The weather was nice and the Sambre looked much nicer than the outward trip but we had now turned onto the Canal Charleroi Brussels. Realised Floreffe would be a good place to stop for the future. We did a mini de-tour into the Canal du Centre then on to Ronquières where we phoned for the two old locks to be opened, Jean-Michel arrived and helped us in. Ian came to collect us and all was left was to clean up the next day, so our Folie would be ready for her next trip. **TOTAL TRIP**: ±1,000 Kilometres 187 Locks and 6 Tunnels.

Home Moorings

CHAPTER TWO - SERIES OF LITTLE TRIPS 1991

After our great adventure last year, many people were eager to have a trip, on the boat so 1991 turned out to be a year of little trips and parties as Deuxième Folie was greeted by family, friends and work colleagues. We had during the early part of the year been working on the boat, of course, a big cleanup was required, and extra bedding brought on board for passengers for the first trip on 19th September. The day before (**18th September**), we left our winter moorings at 19:00 hours and passed the two old locks in preparation, Jacques got back from Holland in time and Bruno joined.

At home, Sue's Mum (Dottie) and her niece Cynth were getting ready to start their voyage. Dottie having finally accepted the fact that we were not giving up our cabin and she had the dropdown dining area made up into a second cabin, Cynth got the short straw on the settee.

Captain's Mum entry on board

<u>19th September</u>. Left at 09:15 hours and into the Plan Incliné, i.e. into the bucket of water, which takes you up on rollers to the top. As it was our second time, we were blasé but Sue's Mum and Cynth were very impressed. Quite a long day, Charleroi was 'smelly' but

when we stopped at Floreffe it was clean again and we were now on the Sambre. Stopped at 20:00 hours having only made the last lock due to the courtesy of the lock keeper, but not thanks to the bargee. Total for the day was twenty-seven kilometres and eight locks.

20ᵗʰ September. Departed at 11:25 hours having first visited the Abbey at Floreffe, quite a climb up which Dottie made, even a ladder but not back! Therefore, Captain had to do a roundabout with the boat to pick her up at the steps, together with Cynth who had kept her company. We were now back on the Meuse and we stopped at Namur for lunch where 45 kids tried to hitch a lift! After lunch, we cruised down the Meuse enjoying the lovely scenery and the ladies loved the houses we passed at Wépion. Around eighteen kilometres and eight locks later, we moored up in Dinant at 18:25 hours.

Beez Marina

21st September. We telephoned to book a mooring at Beez for the following week and then departed around 09:35 hours. Again, the weather was beautiful and we continued on our way to Givet crossing the border and getting rid of the Benelux 5. Did some shopping and Jacques filled the boat with water; repassed the border and got new Benelux 5 valid until March 1992. Moored for the night again at Dinant having passed the same eight locks and another twenty-one kilometres.

22nd September. After the oil change we were enroute – no incidents, the good weather came to an end at the Namur lock but the ladies could enjoy the sun and another look at the beautiful houses with lawns running down to the water's edge. The next stop for Deuxième Folie was at Beez after passing the large lock 'les Grands Malades' where Ian was waiting and we decided it would definitely be a good place to stay in the summer months. Deuxième Folie would stay here until we returned on 27th September. The days total was around twenty kilometres and seven locks. Someone collected us and took us all back.

It was one week later on the **27th September** we arrived with Bruno and his wife Ascension, had supper in Namur, left the car in the parking at Namur Station. Leaving on the morning of **28th September** and with the rain keeping off and we had a good trip to Liege and ended up in the Liege Yacht Harbour, which was a haven of peace and opposite the Church where our marriage was blessed in 1981. Then it was off to the Opera, only three locks, quite a lot of traffic – moored up with Germans and one American. The opera was Il Trovatore with the famous Anvil Chorus and it was very spectacular and also the surroundings of the Palais de Congrès.

After the opera Gilberte & Josette (Bruno's mother and godmother) and Ernesto Grisales, a Spanish opera tenor (who became quite well known) also a working colleague of Bruno's came on board for drinks a perfect end to this excursion.

On the morning of **29th September,** Glenbo (Glenys Zandona a working friend of Sue's) visited and we were taken back to Namur to collect our car and return home.

5th October. Left Liege at 09:00 hours and arrived at Kanne via the Albert Canal.

Entry to Albert Canal

We took Brandy for the first time, and before reaching Kanne, we flooded the boat, so all, well nearly all, of the water Jacques filled up with ended up in the bilge, the bath and the cabin floor. Jacques found CriCri who came on board with Champagne, never went home and sailed with us to Hasselt, having left the house open and no paperwork. Super little yacht basin in Hasselt, only three locks and it was here we were going to leave the boat. First encounter with the Flemish !! 20BF !!. Not sure, who but friends or family picked us up and took us home.

Hasselt

Working with 'days off' again on **1st November** we moved from Hasselt in order to get an early start with the lock at Ham Sluis Kwaadmechalen, already very windy and did not sleep well. Ran the Kubota. On the **2nd November**. The weather was not brilliant but we had been through worse and passed five locks and we went from the Albert Canal to the Canal Beneden Net, then on to the Ruppel, which was tidal. As we were only one hour after high tide, we had no problems. Wind was beginning to make waves, the wind worsened during the night, decided not to move on to Brussels, and left Deuxième Folie moored at "Little Willie" (Willebroek). Again, friends or family came to pick us up and take us home.

On the **8th November,** we finally moved to Brussels, weather not too bad but we had to wait two hours at the Zemst lock, which is an important link on the Brussels-Scheldt sea canal; thank goodness we used the VHF 'illegally'. Arrived at the BRYC, certainly in a better state than the first arrival (see prologue) completely shattered but as we made the dinner dance we could not have been in that bad a state.

9th & 10th November. Two parties were held on board, the first included members of the Royal Naval Association (Captain was Secretary at that time) we were also pleased to have Francois & Paula his wife and son Roger and his wife Isabelle, the guys who got the carcass to float initially. The second party included all our work colleagues from NATO/SHAPE.

28th November. It was time to leave the BRYC and make our back to our home moorings; two friends joined us Sue & Jerry Sarkisian to enjoy the trip. Passed all seven of the locks without problems, the message had been passed and we made it down in the bucket and then through the two small locks where Bruno and Ascension were waiting for us.

On the **29th November,** we moved across the old canal to our permanent mooring where Ghislain was waiting for us. She was the lady who let us put our electricity box on the wall of her house, mentioned in the Prologue.

Therefore, this was the end of 1991's cruising, whilst it was a little stop and start it was not only appreciated by us but many others who joined us. We think that people are now beginning to realise that we may not be completely crazy.

CHAPTER THREE – 1992's TRIPS

10th July. With Deuxième Folie having been prepared earlier with oil/filter gearbox works and cleaning done, we left our permanent moorings with a push! Mud! with the gang. Left the two small locks and then we were stuck again in mud this time really stuck. Luckily a Dutch barge was passing and threw us a rope and pulled us off, we thanked them by sending the rope back with a bottle of whisky attached – much appreciated I am sure, as was their help to us. We had a one hour wait for the 'bucket' and arrived at our pre-destination (Viesville) at 18:50 hours where we would pick up François the next morning.

11th July. Departed at 07:30 hours, François looked like a zombie having had to get up at 03:00 hours in order to find us and get on board. Rough ride through the 'trench' (another name for the smelly stretch) in Charleroi, passing a big barge and following another one at full speed with wash-counter wash and all kind of waves rocked the boat in all directions. We were now on the Sambre being followed by a pleasure boat whose 'captain' was an unpleasant fellow, kicking his wife and child without a minimum of defence. Fortunately, they stopped in Auvelais and we wondered what sort of holiday they would have. We arrived in Namur at 18:00 hours and François had finally enjoyed the boat he had worked on so much.

12th July. Departed at 0800 hours and a short uneventful trip, full use of the VHF, which helped us through the locks, refueled with red fuel on the way (by accident) and arrived in Huy at 12:30 hours where we moored the boat in the Port of Corphalie. Someone again must have picked us up and taken us home.

17th July. We arrived to spend the night on the boat with Sue's Mum (Dottie), for someone who in the past felt sick in the harbour at Dover (UK) was hooked on Deuxième Folie trips. We had to rope the boat to the floating pontoon in order to get her on board via the small ladder! anyone knowing Dottie can imagine the exercise involved!

18th July. Got off to a good start at 0830 hours, but lost one and a half hours at the first lock (Ampsin-Neuville) due to a bargee filling up with water **in the lock**. He went up and down three times before the lock keeper threw him out. The Captain finally moved out between two barges and forced the issue of getting in the Ivoz- Ramet lock. Passed through Liege sitting on the deck in the sun, Dottie with her Croft Sherry and the Captain with her glass of wine, the First Mate was at the helm. We stopped near the Palais des Sports for lunch, after which we continued on and into the Albert Canal going straight this time and not in CriCri, of Hasselt fame's direction. We then passed the Petit Lanage Lock which was fifteen metres moving onto the Juliana Canal alongside the Mass (the Dutch name for the Meuse) and arrived in Maastricht, to find all moorings were full and we had to moor in the countryside – lovely. Met a boatful of Dutch, four children, two adults, one baby, one dog and a small boat.

19th July. Lovely day, finally in the sun we all were burnt, including Dottie. No real problems except the first lock which was meant to be 'open' but was shut because of a regatta and only opened at 10:30 hours. However, we moored with a big barge to whom we gave a bottle for the service, the rest barely said thank you I think they thought it was a bribe but it was just a thank you. The other two locks were also quite large one of fifteen metres and the other thirteen and a half metres. We found a mooring in Wessem and were greeted with "Look there is Deuxième Folie". It was a boat from Ittre (which is nearby Ronquières); they helped us to moor, super mooring with electricity and water, plus boat shop and restaurant.

20th July. Left around 09:00 hours to return to Liege, plenty of big barges on the water and many pleasure boats. One really packed lock and the Captain had to keep the boat on the engine as we could only use one rope. Stopped to shop at GB as we had decided to stay on board for supper. Arrived at Liege found a good mooring but wrong plug for the electricity. Very noisy night with traffic First Mate slept without a problem, even on the roof.

21st July. Marraine duly arrived by train and joined us to Beez. The weather stayed lovely and we had lunch on the deck. We dropped First Mate off at Huy to collect the car. A Dutch married to a Brit who we met in Liege with one problem now had another 'petrol', First Mate took him by car with jerry cans and the problem was solved. The Captain then took off with the ladies and First Mate rejoined us at Andenne where Luc was also waiting with a new girlfriend. Therefore, Luc (Jacques' youngest son) took Marraine home and we left at approximately 19:00 hours to return home with our car.

2nd August. As Deuxième Folie was still in Beez, we took the 'Ladies' i.e. 'The Mums' on a Day trip down the Meuse, little chilly whilst moving but we stopped so the ladies could have a 'ciggie' (only allowed outside of course). We went as far as Wépion, moored up for lunch and returned to Beez in the evening a very pleasant day.

15th August. Well we promised ourselves a relaxed weekend but the day started with bailing out buckets. The conclusion being the rain had got into the boat, we drilled a few more holes (not in the bottom)! with that and the bilge pump, we were able to get ourselves nearly dried out. We left at 1100 hours but lost one hour at the Namur lock and were informed about a 'manifestation' (sailing, ski nautic, etc.). Thus, at Profondville, we were blocked for more than two hours and finally the river police escorted through us. We made Dinant where again we were stopped with a 'soap box on water' competition. All the moorings were full by then so we made another lock still in the company of 'Dagon' also from Beez, they showed us a dear little harbour at Waulsort and we got a visitor's mooring for the price of a sticker! Of course the 15th August is a holiday in Belgium being the Fête de Assumption, a highly religious holy day; but the number of people out and enjoying themselves, were obviously not in Church!

16th August. Left after a good night with only bread and cheese! Had to wait at Anseremme, but arrived back in Dinant exactly at 10:00 hours and Gill Pennington and her friend Chris were waiting, 'then it was all aboard and back again through the Anseremme lock, we were beginning to know it! Cruised up to Hastière, had lunch and turned back to Dinant and yes again through Anseremme, locking through this time with a large pleasure craft. We 'poured' Gill off and Chris was to drive them home, a very safe idea. Again no mooring space in Dinant, so back again through the Anseremme lock and moored up at a super mooring run by Dinant, just after the lock, the one that had been full the night before. All mod coms electricity/water and a good restaurant nearby.

17th August. Left around 09:30 hours back through the now, famous Anseremme lock where we were made to feel like old friends. We locked all the way to Namur with four Dutch and one 'puddle jumper' with a very young girl with a young man, Stopped at Namur for a couple of hours and then back to Beez by 17:30 hours What a lovely weekend except for a short shower this morning beautiful weather all the time. Our car was here awaiting us to go home.

Now it was time to move Deuxième Folie back to her winter moorings as we were doing this at the beginning of November we were not sure how the weather would be. The Captain left Beez alone around 09:00 hours on **7th November**, the sun appeared but not for long. The boat was very humid but it had been left idle for nearly three months and with the rain, it was hardly surprising, thus, we found another compartment full of water. Jacques took the car to Marraine's and left it in the hangar, so by the time I arrived at Andenne he had made it back on foot. We continued to move on to Maastricht uneventfully; except we arrived in the dark at 17:45 hours, we had forgotten it was winter! We could however moor up in town, which was impossible during the high season.

On the **8th November,** we took a day off, ran the engine and the generator and lunched at the Maastricht Hotel, lovely sunny day. The **9th November** proved to be an important day NO BENELUX 5 but we passed Customs at Mermans and he noted our passage. Then horrors they wanted 4,000 BF to use two locks on a 'Flemish' canal 'Zuid-willem svaart'. After a lengthy discussion and a bottle of whisky, we were let off. Very heavy winds refueled and now on the Albert Canal until joining the Meuse and eventually arrived in Liege at 17:00 hours

On the **10th November,** we left Liege at 10:00 hours, stopped to shop – wine of course. Winds still quite high but Deuxième Folie stood up to the buffeting very well. We locked through with ESME who pushed at the last lock but did not leave us completely behind so they had to wait at the last lock for us. We travelled for the second time in the dark for around two hours. Very impressive especially on entry into Namur. We moored up alongside the restaurant boats. As the **11th November** was a holiday, we did not move but ran the engine in order to get some heat, terrible day rain and high winds. Christiane Dispas (who was an old family friend of Jacques and living in Namur) came and we went out to lunch on one of the neighbouring boats – excellent.

The **12th November** saw us leaving Namur at 08:45 hours onto the Sambre but lost one hour at the first lock, which was only ten minutes away! locked through with a French barge. Had to wait for one lock to be cleared of floating wood but finally got ahead – we thought – passed the first lock before Charleroi, entered into the town that was awful as usual. A lot of works on-going on the sides, we made the next lock in town only to find out that it was 17:30 hours closure not 18:00 hours. We pushed like hell and arrived with fifteen minutes to spare, just our luck there was a large barge in it, which eventually exited, but with five minutes to closing, they shut the doors!! Therefore, we turned around, crossed to the other side – in the dark again, and moored at Dampremy.

The **13th November** we moved on, filling up with fuel on the way – no problems except on arrival at Ronquières could not make contact via phone, eventually another barge arrived and the lock keeper woke up! The wind was terrible, front battery died and with it the bow prop, made it into the lock and had just enough juice to get out elegantly. Gill Pennington (who had been on dog duty at La Folie) was waiting and joined Bruno's godmother and us on board, Gill not well so went back to get Sue's car. In-between we were trying to find a lock keeper to get us into our mooring through the two small locks. Although we were there at 14:00 hours, we moored finally in the dark and after a deluge!

SAD 1993

For personal reasons and work commitments it meant the Deuxième Folie was left alone on her local moorings, how we longed for retirement. Our life with Deuxième Folie was interrupted after purchasing the Troisème Folie nearby the Canal du Midi at Ségala. Our thoughts were already to the move of Deuxième Folie down to the Canal du Midi on our retirement and what a trip that will be.

CHAPTER FOUR

29th APRIL – 20th MAY 1994

After an enforced break from Deuxième Folie mentioned above, it was a big clean up with help from Vivianne (from the local Café in Henripont and also my cleaner), I love my thirty-two windows but cleaning them is no fun and it usually rains after I have done it. We left on **29th April 1994** with ten passengers and one wet dog (Brandy) who fell into the second little lock and had to be hauled out via the ladder in the wall. The passengers were all eager to take a ride up the Plan Incliné, we missed the first 'bucket' so had to wait one hour, then we eventually passed in the company of a scrap metal barge and four other pleasure crafts. Visitors were duly dropped off at the top having thoroughly enjoyed the experience. Weather was incredible First Mate's face is already brown.

Beloved Brandy

We had filled up with water in the morning so when we stopped, probably at Viesville, we were ready for a shower – NO WATER!! we opened the floor and there it all was in the bilge, now we have to find out how it got there – faulty water pump? Serves our right for ignoring her for one year. Thus, already a change of direction as we would have to go back to Beez and were unable to move on the Sunday as four locks were not working due to flood damage on the Meuse.

Locked through with 'Dahlia' (a lovely small barge) having got ready for an early start at 08:00 hours start on **30th April** as the locks close early today at 1800 hours due to the 1st of May holiday. We just made Namur, well we did not just, and we had to wait for the four yachts we left behind at the first lock. Still no water! As after the floods, no electricity or water points working in Namur and because of the early closure we could not make Beez so just moored up in town regardless. We will have to see if the locks are working downstream tomorrow otherwise we will have to visit Christiane with empty water bottles, other than the water problem, everything was fine and Brandy was settling down, but we thought she might be missing the other dogs. They were probably not missing her it was a bit like the third child with Brandy being the third dog.

1st May. Our luck was in – the locks were working downstream. So after a visit to the flea market, bread, water etc. we moved around 10:00 hours to Beez, we were greeted like old friends and the Captain made an excellent mooring. The First Mate worked on the water problem, but we need a spare part, but being the great Mate he is he by-passed the system, we were full of water again and had a bath! Brandy not happy with the floating pontoon, we had to lift her off but eventually she could get back on.

We left Beez around 08:00 hours on **2nd May** and the first lock was ready, we passed Namur and the second lock opened by the time we arrived at the fourth lock we found a flotilla accumulated at the entrance. This was the start of four locks badly damaged in the floods (Rivieère, Hun, Houx and Dinant); the doors had to be dragged open by a tractor. Overall, we locked through with ten other boats of varying types and sizes and the time passed quietly in the sun. The last two the doors were opened by a 'lorry' but as there was only one lorry doing both locks we had to sit and wait for one and a half hours in the lock awaiting its return. First Mate badly sun burnt, the Captain's tough old skin was OK but even so a little red. We stopped at Dinant for shopping then did one more lock alone and moored up for the night at Anseremme around 17:30 hours the pontoon had been mended but no water or electricity due to the flooding, the damage had been quite considerable but in the sun, it was hard to imagine. We knew about the floods, had checked France, and had stupidly forgot to check Belgium.

Moved off on **3rd May** from Anseremme around 08:30 hours passed three locks to arrive at Givet, refueled, had lunch and finally bought a frying pan (Captain forgot it) so we had our eggs and bacon! We kept meeting some of the boats from the flotilla, Sweet Sue and Sun Ray to mention just two. During our shopping, we also bought pliers and a screwdriver, the Captain was not the only one to forget something. Passed into France at 14:00 hours no borders, no more paperwork problems, then into the first of the small locks (les trois

Fontaines) followed by a tunnel (hit the sides twice sounded worse than it was). Two more locks (Mouyon and Montigny) at the third (Fépin) we were told problems ahead at the next lock, sure enough two inside one across the entrance and they were waiting for the fire brigade. We decided to backtrack, as it was already 17:30 hours and moored at a campsite's private mooring, lovely spot and no one but us near the pont de Haybes. We eventually saw a fire truck pass on the other side so it will be interesting to see what we find tomorrow morning.

Having left at 08:50 hours on the **4th May** and the sun was with us but not completely, we eventually moored up just outside Charleville Mézieres at 20:00 hours! One of those days, we could not find a suitable mooring, made more difficult because of Brandy and we were having a taste of our first rain. The heavens opened just, as usual, as we arrived in a lock. We saw some good moorings in the morning and noted them on the maps. We were given a 'gadget' to open the automatic locks, they were not all working correctly but a lock keeper was available; this is still all a result of the floods. We did one tunnel, which the First Mate did perfectly.

5th May. Much easier day today, spurts of sunshine, cloudy, a little rain but nothing much. We left our delectable little mooring outside the lock around 08:15 hours and entered in, then headed for the 'automatic' which we thought was working then we found a lock keeper who helped us with the ropes, difficult lock (No 43 – Montcy at pont-à-Bar). Passed another three and we turned into the first one on the Canal des Ardennes, passing without problems in the place where we were stuck in the mud in 1991. Still mud there and still no warning and it was the same lock keeper who remembered us. Continued without problems mooring up at Le Chesne (water and electricity) at 16:00 hours there were two other boats there, both British. Did some shopping and phoned, an also ate out for the first time – not bad and Brandy was excellent.

The next day, **6th May**, left a little later at 09:00 hours but the weather had by this time had turned to drizzle and remained dull all day which was a shame because the countryside was lovely and would have been so much better in the sun. It was the day of the twenty-six automated locks, lost and recovered one fender (courtesy of lock keeper on moped), one lock failed to open ended in mud and First Mate was screaming at the Captain – defaulters tomorrow. Completed the locks in five and three quarter hours not bad going. We spent the night at Rethel nice mooring but electricity and water not yet switched on.

What a difference the sun makes and all on the **7th May,** it stayed with us having departed around 09:00 hours then passing eight locks to Berry-au-Bac. Enroute we started some heavy deck cleaning scrubbing with brush and Cif. Our next change of direction took us on to the Canal l'Aisne à la Marne that would take us to Reims. We entered into another section of nine automated locks, slow but interesting. We picked up our first 'hitchhikers' a grandmother and her two granddaughters who we took from one lock to the next where she lived – quite amusing! We eventually arrived at Reims at 2000 hours having had a problem with the last lock, which necessitated a call for a lock keeper.

As we were back to rain we spent another day in Reims, did the washing at the Capitanerie, ate out, Brandy was excellent as usual and we had a taste of champagne. We were determined to stop this time as last time we did not.

On the morning of the **9th May,** before we moved to the refueling point to top up we went for a champagne breakfast – that is the way to do it. Eventually got on the way at noon and the sun was shining. We backtracked down the automated locks, busier today with commercial traffic and it took us three and a half hours. We then turned port into the Canal Latéral à l'Aisne et l'Aisne canalisé scenery lovely, especially as the sun was still with us. The second large fender was ripped – one each now! We continued with the external cleaning of the boat just the roof left. We moored up in the countryside and barbequed but noted that at Vailly-sur-Aisne there was moorings a café and restaurant, for future reference.

The morning of **10th May,** we woke up to a mist, so were lazy and left at 10:00 hours after the sun came through. Lovely day only went through three locks one double (Celles) and one single (Villeneuve), met one barge and stopped in Soissons around noon. Nice moorings but not finished yet so no water or electricity. We went around the town, which had been badly damaged in the 14/18 war; although the Cathedral had been re-built, it looked dilapidated. Cooked on board. Saw the eclipse. Good shopping, launderette and First Mate saved a Labrador some stupid woman let swim in the Aisne, he was exhausted and had to be helped out and wrapped in one of our towels, and he was OK. Due to Brandy's fall at the start of the trip, she had no interest in water any more – thank goodness.

The **11th May** saw us leaving around 08:50 hours again in the sun, continuing down the Aisne, really beautiful scenery; obviously, there is money here as some of the houses with their own moorings and boathouses were super. Saw a little traffic, i.e. four barges, one private yacht and a pleasure boat. We looked for the moorings by the Railway Carriage but they no longer existed and we carried on to Compiegne and stayed at the same little port we had used three years previously, some of the people were the same and recognized Deuxième Folie. It is a lovely town and a lot of work had been done making pedestrian areas.

The **12th May** was cloudy during the morning after the overnight rain but cleared up and we were again in the sun. We changed course again and moved on to the Oise saw quite a few barges for Ascension Day, we then changed again to St. Quentin and all locks were automated only one did not work and a lock keeper arrived to push the buttons. We moored up in the countryside but walked to the village of Jussy, which had a very strange church.

Left on the morning of the **13th May** around 09:30 hours again in the sun and passed through the automatic locks to the junction of the Canal de la Sambre. This was classed as 'neglected' and there was certainly nowhere to stop and very shallow in places 0.5! however, very interesting, some manual locks saw one small yacht named 'Great Escape' which was British with only one man in sight. We then went on to join the Canal de Nord and met the commercial traffic again. The next locks were not automated, at one the First Mate had to climb up the ladder in the wall – 9 metres!, we locked through with a barge and then stopped at a Port de Plaisance at Peronne. Excellent – water, electricity, washing machine, shops etc. was adjacent to a caravan site and well maintained. We managed to B-B-Q but had to eat inside due to a heavy storm.

The rain stayed with us the next day **14 May** our first full day of rain for some time and although we left around 09:00 hours heading for Amiens we had to moor up amongst canoeists, there was a 24-hour 'canoe-in' presumably for charity. We were now on the Somme and it was lovely incredible marshes and you realised that WW1 must have been under difficult conditions. I hope that it is sunny tomorrow and we can take some photos. We imagined it must be a fisherman's paradise, as we had never seen so many. The locks in this stretch varied from 3 metres to 1 metre so not so strenuous for the First Mate. Moving into Amiens was fascinating many little canals with gardens called the 'Floating Gardens' never seen anything like it. The stream was very fast which made mooring difficult, that plus the canoeists. One other boat 'Stourmaid' was moored and came to help us, they were British and came on board later for a drink. We then had a deluge never seen such rain and we were leaking badly through one of the skylights and we eventually ate supper with a towel as a tablecloth. In addition to the normal locks, we passed under three bridges that worked with a weigh system, another first for Deuxième Folie.

The **15th May** we were back to the sun and after a visit to the Amiens Cathedral, we left with the canoeists at 10:30 hours, and managed to film the things we saw in the rain and the day progressed peacefully until we reached Lock 13 (Sailly). The doors were open but so were the vannes (sluices) with the resultant rush of water. With the aid of passer-byes and three ropes, we tied up. No lock keeper in sight and the lock had no ladder and was three metres in depth and we were trying to go up. The First Mate did some gymnastics with our ladder/plank on the roof and managed to climb out. He stopped the flow of water (illegally) searched for a lock keeper after forty minutes we gave up and the First Mate manipulated the lock himself. The next lock (Méricourt), again manual and again no lock keeper, but as the First Mate had all the tools at the ready, he again did his job with a crowd of onlookers, as usual. We then arrived at the next manual (Froissy) again not a person in sight, luckily one lock keeper arrived home, he phoned the duty one who eventually took us through the next two manuals to Cappy where we moored up at 17:30 hours way behind schedule. The lock keeper came on board for a drink and told us that he eventually got the message but by the time he had got to Lock 13 we were long gone. Although time lost, it was lost in sun and beautiful scenery.

16 May – apparently, it thundered last night – we heard nothing! it was a very quiet place and conducive to sleep. We weighed anchor at 09:10 hours and our little man opened the first of the three bridges and we passed smoothly up the Somme, small amount of traffic but as we joined the Canal du Nord that all changed. With its big locks of six metres and then the tunnel!! (Ruyarlcourt 4,354 metres long), the Captain could not cope with this and the First Mate took over doing an excellent job. There was a passing point in the middle with traffic lights where an enormous empty barge was alongside us in the dark like a phantom, very frightening and the forty minutes it took to go through seemed like a lifetime. Captain took over again and the First Mate had earned his rum ration. Having got to the top it was down again through another seven six-plus metre locks, not for the feint hearted or amateurs. We moored up at a little 'Halte Fluviale' exhausted at 19:15 hours.

Off we were on the **17th May** at 09:30 hours with one lock left on the Canal de Nord, which was nine metres. We then headed for Douai where we thought we had picked up the 'Scarpe', very pretty area and very small and then a bridge appeared that should not have been there which told us that for the first time we had missed a turning. Luckily, we found a place wide enough to turn Deuxième Folie around and finally did enter the Scarpe, which is not used much, and the staffing was not good. We had to wait one hour for a lock keeper who then proceeded to push us like a rocket through the remaining bridges and locks. The weather was dull with the sun popping out every now and then, but it was a longer day than intended as we had difficulties in finding a suitable mooring. In the end, we moored just before the junction of the Scarpe/Escaut Canal de Mons at Montagne-du-Nord.

We woke up on the **18th May** to a foggy morning so went shopping, filled up with water and did set off until 12:30 hours the lock keeper had been to see if we were OK. The fog lifted, although not completely, we did catch a sight of the sun. We continued on the Escaut as far as Tournai – quite impressive but suitable for pleasure boats the 'Pont Notre Dame' was very impressive and surprisingly the Ronquières sightseeing boat was moored there. Turned back towards the Canal Nimy Blaton-Peronnes. Two locks, one of which was twelve and a half metres, unfortunately something in the water – unseen – and the bow-prop went; luckily, we are nearing the end of the trip. Moored up in the countryside, small quay recommended by the lock keeper at Antoing.

19 May we thought would be our last day, turned out not to be. The day started with a long stretch, which took us to the Grand Large Mons. Something seen from a different angle, then on past the big locks and Obourg Ciment; again seeing things from the other side.

The new canal had been started swing bridge, a lock gone, and a new lock taking us to the first of the famous lifts (Thieu, Hordeng-Aimeries, and Houdeng-Goegnies). The four hydraulic boatlifts on this short stretch of the historic Canal du Centre are industrial monuments of the highest quality. Together with the canal itself and its associated structures, they constitute a remarkably well preserved and complete example of a late-19th-century industrial landscape. Of the eight hydraulic boat-lifts built at the end of the 19th and beginning of the 20th century, the only ones in the world which still exist in their original working condition are these four lifts on the Canal du Centre. These are twinned with the Anderton Lock in the UK. A new enormous lift is now being created but will not be finished until 2002 so we obviously never get to use it.

One of the Lifting Locks

It was also quite spectacular passing bridges being lifted. The last swing bridge broke down and whilst it was being repaired, the Captain used her initiative to replenish the wine. The last lift was industrial and the water looked like ink. Arrived at Ronquières and after five minutes we took the last bucket down for the night.

20ᵗʰ May. After a phone call, we arranged our entry through the two small locks to our mooring. The two old guys came on board for drinks, Jean-Claude (he was the guy who helped us to install and get acceptance of the electricity metre mention in the Prologue) to read the electricity metre, and by 13:00 hours we were back at our home mooring.

<u>TOTAL TRIP</u>: 875 Kilometres – 204 Locks – 20 Bridges – 4 Tunnels

CHAPTER FIVE - Series of Short Trips

<u>**1995**</u>

1st July. The Captain arrived with Vivianne, already mentioned above and we got the boat ready, because of the heat we were early, at the request of the lock keeper, entered the first of the old locks at 09:00 hours, and left it at 10:00 hours. There were problems with the doors and divers had to be called in and a bicycle was recovered, we then moved and eventually moored up near the pleasure boat at 11:00 hours. The Captain then returned home to load the car up with the rest of the gear, returned loaded the boat and was relaxing in swimsuit with a drink in hand when The First Mate finally arrived at 13:30 hours. We then rushed home again left one car, got Brandy returned and suddenly realised we had to move. There was a lot of traffic so we were in the bucket without our guests, they caught up with us at the top and we moored so they could at least come on board for a drink. Beautiful evening and we cruised to Viesville, another one of our favourite stopping places mooring up at 17:30 hours and the evening was terminated with a lovely BBQ.

2nd July. Off we went around 08:30 hours enroute for Beez, not many problems, fair amount of traffic but it was hot! no wind not even when moving. Ended up from Charleroi to Namur with a barge that was pushing but he ended up having to wait for us! because it was so hot, we had given the lock keepers a drink and at the end gave the bargee a bottle, as he had been so patient! Surprise! he refused and said if we gave it, he would throw it in the water, in hindsight we think he thought we had been bribing the lock keepers to wait for us with the drinks. Second time this has happened so another experience chalked up. We arrived at Beez around 17:30 hours nice mooring as usual with water and electricity. We left the boat here until our return on ninth and some kind soul collected us and took us back to our car.

9th July. We collected two grandsons (Gregory and Alexis) and we were finally off on a voyage that had been promised to them for ages. We moved upstream through Namur, Dinant and intended to stop at Anseremme but it was packed everywhere, so we ended up mooring in the countryside right opposite Fryer Castle, which was known for its beautiful gardens, quite an impressive mooring. Not our first time in this area and certainly not the last. Gregory had a hissy fit about mozzies and none of us got much sleep.

10th July. We started back in the morning and the boys were really good – no mozzies in sight! Stopped at Dinant, got some bread and we had a problem with 'fast boats' and one stupid canoeist with a child balanced in front of him. Then the first of the noises started, we reversed thinking it was a plastic, seemed better, but got worse and we crawled back to Beez; the boys had at least had their outing. We drove back home and then returned on the **17th July.** Luc came ready to dive! which he did 'chapeau' in the dirty Meuse; there was no apparent problem with the rudder. As Nathalie and her parents had joined so we went for a little trip. Had to moor up and inspect under the floor and the First Mate replaced one joint but there is obviously a big problem. Not to spoil the day we went slowly through Namur and a couple of locks and back to Beez, now realising that she would have to be taken out of the water.

21st July. Well we chugged off from Beez at a speed of eighteen being our comfortable speed, first lock slow due to a trainee; it took us one and a half hours to arrive just before the turning to the Sambre – NO TRANSMISSION. Luckily, a Dutch converted barge had forced us under the far right arch of the bridge so with the stream and the rudder we could tie up. Three hours later with the help of a bargee the First Mate mended it by replacing the pin and guess what we were back to normal speed, the broken pin must have caused all the problems. However, the problems were not over as two locks later the 'temporary drill bit' replacement snapped - NO TRANSMISSION AGAIN. This time with the aid of the lock keeper, we sawed off a screwdriver and two hours later, we were off again and could make the next lock.

22nd July. It held and the screwdriver is still in place, this was to be a long day having entered the first lock at 06:30 hours not too many delays, filled up with 100 litres of fuel, a pleasure boat 'ELGERIA' missed the turning to Brussels and then the delays started! Waited two hours outside the first of the big three – there were many pleasure boats and when we eventually arrived at Ronquières we found out why – a STRIKE at Lanahaye on the Meuse direction of Holland so everyone had to come through here. There were fifteen queued for the morning, some already have been waiting for three hours, it was the time of the charbon being moved by barges as well. The First Mate chatted with one of the lock keepers who told us we should move since pleasure boats had right of way. Unless you knew this the bargee's would push ahead, the Captain thus took the initiative and moved to the head of the queue. We made the last bucket having picked Luc & Nathalie on the way, with guess who, the Elgiria boat, the cause of all our initial delays.

23rd July. Off we were on the last stage to the BRYC for the repairs, Ronquières did not see us leave so Ittre did not know we were coming. Therefore, the first wait of the day, 'Hoppity' was on duty and we bought our 'sticker' and got away with 1,000 BF, the trip was uneventful, and the screwdriver held. We only had one more wait and that was for the bridge coming into Brussels, we think he had fallen asleep, arrived at the BRYC and Alain the person in charge was there so moored up safely and she is ready to be taken out on Wednesday morning the **27th July**.

This is where things get a little hazy as we did not keep a record of the time spent at the BRYC and additionally the Captain did not make a log of the return trip, naughty Captain. People did help us and I do not think I will ever forget Tony van Gossum who turned into a Smuf whilst sanding off the blue anti-fouling. It was certainly a couple of months, so we probably took it back near the end of the year, with work commitments it was probably November using holidays and/or a weekend to do so.

One thing I did not forget was that the First Mate fell in the drink when we got home (i.e.

we were moored), the Captain was cleaning inside and realised he was missing, shouted out 'Where are you' and the reply came back very quickly 'In the bloody drink!'. The Captain rushed to the rescue saw the rope he was hanging on to and pulled with all her might only did not realise it was wrapped around his feet. Therefore, every time she pulled it he disappeared under, luckily Charlie was duty lock keeper, saw what happened and rushed to pull him out correctly. No damage done and he was fine after a good glass of wine and a change of clothes!

1996

19th July we finally moved Deuxième Folie out with a full house as usual for a trip in the bucket, all family this time Chantal with her four, Ian & Melissa and their two (Sean and CJ). No one fell in but Gregory stayed on board to work on his Math's with his granddad moored at Viesville, as already mentioned a favourite stop for us and had a BBQ.

Grandson Gregory

20th July we had decided to take it easy and not push to Andenne, we were ready for the off with the First Mate preparing the ropes, Captain started the engine, NO START. Down into the depths again had to move the steps and had to saw off a couple of wooden planks. Nothing! We then phoned François – BATTERIES, sure enough dead as a dodo – BOTH. Well good old Ian was at home so phoned explained where we were and within one hour, he was with us together with jumper cables! it must be the first time on record that a Renault V jump-started a boat.

Renault V 'Jump Start'

So we were finally off enjoying the lovely weather, got to last bend before the lock NO RUDDER, Captain controlled the boat excellently. So off we were again with running repairs, only this time we had to move the settee, problem quickly solved put the pin back in, obviously, when it had been replaced during its stay in dry dock the pin had not been opened, just put in. Off we were again and got to the lock to find it was broken so La Louvière for the night and 09:00 hours start in the morning. We are getting the feeling that Deuxième Folie is getting her own back on us for being neglected!

21st July was, surprise surprise basically a day without incident but not according to plan. We passed the lifts coming the other way, still lovely, the new lift is really growing although finishing date is 31 December 1999 (it was actually 2002 before it was finished as mentioned above). Maybe a way to spend the millennium we thought at the time? Mooring in Mons on the Grande Large proved difficult due to the speedboats, water skiers etc. etc. therefore, we moored up at a different place. Good old Ian came and got the Captain and now we have a car at both ends. Chantal did not arrive until 20:00 hours to collect Gregory – again a long hot day and the mozzies were in full swing.

22nd July. Well Deuxième Folie had her first British Admiral on Board, Mike Gretton together with Bob Giacomo and his wife Eddie. Collection of them went well, unfortunately, the old Wren was not able to pipe him on board, and we set off on a return trip again through the five lifts already mentioned before and culminating with Ronquières. No real incidents except never let Admirals loose on little boats so the tally for the day was one lost/recovered fender and one blown up! Captain lost one fender (due to wind and not bad steering) then the other one was down to that Admiral. At the office the next day a replacement fender arrived on the Captain's desk with a yellow ribbon around it – general feeling was a good historical trip, may be hysterical might be a better word.

Admiral Mike Gretton

4th August. Just a little trip to Ittre to fill the water tanks NO ENGINE again battery definitely dead! This time a jump-start with the Renault Espace – not as efficient as the Renault V. We finally succeeded – met up with 'Hoppity' who came on board for drink at the lock whilst we filled up. Busy little trip with the speedboats etc. however, we have our quittance ready for next trip.

14th August. The Captain loaded the boat including Dottie, checked with Ronquières about a possible departure around 1730-1745 hours – 'Very Unlikely'. So quick phone call to First Mate and he and Sue Hanneker left NATO at 15:30 hours and we moved towards the bucket around 17:00 hours. In the end perfect timing and we had the bucket to ourselves and against all odds the sun was out. We dropped Sue Hanneker off at her car and we continued to La Louvière for the night, ready for the five lifts in the morning.

15th August moved through the lifts, which are on the Canal Blaton-Ath with problems and then it changed into the Dendre where we had intended spending the night. Suddenly the lock keeper appeared; we had no choice, so we hit the first of ten locks. Good choice, we spent the night with cows, fishermen and Dottie! moreover, after a BBQ, we all had a good night.

16th August. The locks started at 08:00 hours apparently a moped passed us and told the lock keeper we were up! We are in the sun and in the wilds, we had one speedy lock keeper and we rescued a pigeon in a lock with the aid of 'tinet' (this is a small bucket with a rope tied to it, normally used to get water from the canal to throw over the boat for cleaning purposes). We hope the way back is less rushed.

17th August. We started slowly having to ring the bell for the swing bridge and then wait one hour at the first lock. After we got going, we actually passed back down the ten locks in two hours and we were then back to the wide canal and on to Mons. Andre's 'Arcadis' was doing his tourist bit and confirmed our suspicions no fuel available on the canal. Therefore, we moored up at Nimy and the First Mate lugged 5 x 20 litres by jerry can, he was exhausted. That evening he went to bed early and slept and the Captain tried to be helpful but ended up dropping the Kubota (the generator) in the 'flotte' trying to get it back on board but ended up breaking the wooden railing and falling in the drink in the dark at 22:30 hours! Got out eventually, after swimming around looking for a ladder in the wall to climb out soggy but none the worse for the wear. However, lot of panic on board, especially from Dottie (first time I heard her use a really bad swear word) the First Mate was just angry with the Captain for disobeying his orders and waking him up!

18th August. I suppose this weekend will be put down as not one of the most successful. We were ready by 09:00 hours went into the first lock at 09:30 hours finally going up the first lift one and a half hours later. We thought that was it we made it to the last lift – BROKEN DOWN – might be repaired tomorrow. We finally contacted Eric & Marie-Danielle (our neighbours), they came to get us, Dottie, and First Mate went back, the Captain waited for him to return with our car, and then we cleared out the boat. Happy Days.

Here there is another blank in the logbook, because obviously we went back at some point and moved Deuxième Folie back to her mooring and repaired what had to be repaired. These little trips taking place when we had a few days around a holiday off from work, and/or on a weekend as usual.

14 September. We left for a little day trip with seven passengers (l'équip du restaurant de l'OTAN), weather passable. Due to a late start, we did a little trip towards Ittre and then back for the bucket, all amazed as usual. We went to look at the works on the new canal then moored up for lunch (provided à l'italiene – Antonio and the équip). We had seen Michel Winders (Marie-Danielle's brother) with his speedboat, he tied up alongside and had a drink and then took five of our party for a fast spin, including Gia who was seven and a half months pregnant. They returned on board whilst both boats were moving. The bucket was down so we had to wait and then went through with 'Mayrse' another pleasure boat who's Captain came onboard for a look-see. Our visitors left us having really enjoyed they day out and the "boys" were waiting at the old locks – one blocked, eventually cleared by First Mate this time and we moored up at the old landing and will put her to bed tomorrow.

15 September. Well here, we are back in place and of course, the sun is shining. The new mooring planks look very smart, hopefully they will last better. This was the end of 1996 for the boat roll on 1997.

1997

1st August was the first little move out of the two small locks, which only seem to be used only by us now; it was uneventful except we seemed to have no neutral? We took the two mooring planks with us and moored up under the bridge ready for the off tomorrow.

2nd August we left at 12:00 hours having been very efficient in loading the boat etc. Saw the bucket starting to move so drove home dropped off one car and returned with the Renault V. The engine started straight away and off we were into the bucket for once alone and had the bucket to ourselves. The view from the top never ceases to amaze us and we slowly moved on to Montignies on the Sambre where we spent the evening and night not quite making the last lock.

The **3rd August** saw us back in Beez having moved with three Dutch barges, they tried to out run us – but they had to wait. Once in the Marina we connected to the electricity, shut up shop and Luc arrived to take us, unfortunately, back home.

12th August. Unexpected outing due to a certain Colonel Piers Bateman, who decided to have a 'Character Building' sport-type afternoon. To cut a long story short, the Captain's Office closed and we were enroute to Namur, together with Johan, Ken & Joy and Sylvia (my Aunt who was visiting together with Jo her daughter-in-law). We would have left in good time if the organiser had not been late. Anyway, we had enough time for a good outing with super sun, a good time was had by all, and Piers got some Brownie Points for the champagne.

Character Building

15 August was a Belgian holiday with lovely weather so we could not resist another little outing on the Meuse. Luc, Nathalie and Max came with us and Max was excellent and wore his yellow jacket without complaints, Sylvia was still with us and enjoyed the trip but Jo had opted to stay at home and sunbathe! We sailed as far as Poilvache, which is a ruined medieval castle on the top overlooking the village of Houx; we did not pass Ecluse 5 (Houx) and returned to Beez nicely browned.

Grandson Max

27 September. Unfortunately, we had to start back to our winter moorings, we eventually left Beez around noon, after breakfast with Marraine, and the fog had lifted. Lovely sun and no incidents, locked through with one small barge and after an uneventful trip moored for the night just after Roselies.

28 September. Still very foggy when we left so navigation lights were the order of the day. This is always the worst part of the trip through the industrial area. Then after passing the three large locks, we had around thirty-five kilometres to Ronquières by ourselves with the sun now shining brightly. Heavenly! Phoned ahead to Ronquières and the bucket was there waiting for us. Drinks onboard with the duty lock keeper, awaiting the final move through the two old locks and Deuxième Folie would be tucked up for the winter.

At the beginning of 1998, we took the decision to retire, starting our retirement on **1ˢᵗ April 'All Fool's Day'** – done on purpose to keep our life full of Follies. This was to be the biggest adventure of our lives to enter into retirement in line with our planning; which planning the majority of our family, friends, acquaintances at NATO and SHAPE never thought would happen and probably quite a few thought we were mad or 'Follies'.

CHAPTER SIX 1998 - ANCHORS AWEIGH TOWARDS TROISIEME FOLIE

20 April. We were finally ready for the great depart, a trip estimated to take us five to six weeks moving Deuxième Folie to her new home on the Canal du Midi, France on the Esplanade Le Ségala. Belgium was saying goodbye to us in the only way it could, by raining. Some friends, Geneviève and Gerard (Delaite) and Jean from the Belle Vue came with us up the 'bucket' nostalgically for us as it would be the last time we would be using it. Jean an avid photographer was clicking like mad the whole way, he had been composing a history of the Plan Incliné and realised the only photos he did not have were from the water.

Ronquières

We arrived at the junction with the AutoRoute where we let our passengers off, the first mishap the First Mate managed to break a window in the door; mind you, the doors had been the bain of our lives from the beginning letting in so much water so we stuck some tape across the crack and boldly continued. We passed the seven-metre locks and made the refueling station at Marchienne-au-Pont on the Sambre.

The water was running extremely fast, the Captain touched the floating Church, said a quick prayer but moved on, nearest thing to a hit, and run, I suppose. At the next lock, the Captain burst a fender; that we were a little rusty was a certainty. Despite the weather, we progressed better than anticipated, especially as we had to wait over an hour at Ronquières at the start; we eventually moored up for the night at Auvelais on the Sambre.

21 April. This turned out to be a heavy day, due to torrential rainfalls and traffic; the barges that had been held up due to the bad weather were now all on the move. The Sambre continued to run extremely fast and Deuxième Folie took quite a hammering, but stood up to the test. We turned into the Meuse at Namur and actually made our intended destination Anseremme, even though we had to wait some forty-five minutes at La Plante but we were lucky to pass, as there had been considerable restrictions until mid-day due to the weather conditions. It so lovely to move on the Meuse out of season with no hassle from speedboats and water skiers we would really enjoy the scenery and savour the freedom of retirement with no thoughts of having to return to work. We arrived at Anseremme without any more delays and we received our first visitors Mike & Fran Turner who live in Anseremme, how he copes with the daily journey to NATO from there we could not imagine, it used to kill us doing it from Braine-le-Comte.

22 April. The Captain went off for coffee with Fran and the First Mate stayed to change the oil and filter. On return having finished his jobs we set off around 11:00 hours with the Meuse to ourselves in the sunshine with friendly lock keepers and all locks ready for us. We crossed into France with a final 'cheap' refueling at Givet and felt that now we had really started the trip with the certainty that we would not be sailing the Belgian waterways again. At the lock keepers suggestion, we moored up for the night at Fumay, with its new moorings, water, electricity and Capitainerie – with all facilities. This proved to be a wise decision.

After securing our ropes, the First Mate plugged in our little generator and it blew up, resulting in soot all over the bridge. Then the loo broke, followed by the shower. Therefore, there would be no early start tomorrow just running repairs. That night was spent with no shower and a plastic bucket balancing on the bath as the only 'pee' facilities.

23 April. Lovely morning and thanks to the Capitainerie we were able to shower and do some washing, sun beautiful so it all dried. That was the upside, the down side was that the loo was still not mended and our intended departure at 14:00 hours was definitely not on. However, luck was on our side, because of a 'Frite Stand', we were at that point feeling a little dejected when the Captain saw a plumber's van by the frite stand and sent the First Mate rushing to accost him. Always quick to obey his Master off he went and after rummaging in the back of the van with the plumber, the dismantling of two taps (still not sure what they had to do with the loo) came back with the spare part. The First Mate then got in his exercise by cycling to the next lock to tell the keeper that we were sorry we would not make it today and our estimated time was now 09:00 hours the next day. Loo had now been mended and no plastic bucket was required.

24 April. Weather changed to drizzle by the time we left at 09:00 hours, it cleared up a little and we saw the sun but certainly not brilliant. The scenery was still lovely but the stream sill very fast in places. We moved into the automated lock system with our personal little gadget this was certainly more up market than the last time we had passed that way. I have distinct memories of dropping the First Mate on shore with a frying pan trying to activate one of them. We had one tunnel during the day (at Revin – no lights so floodlight required) - which the Captain did expertly. It was a single lane controlled upstream by the lock keeper and downstream you had to ring a cord in order to get permission to enter.

We moored up at Château Regnault, small but with water and electricity and as it seemed were the only ones on the water there was no problem; could imagine in high season it was a much sought after place. The statue of 'Les Quatre fils Aymon' stood on the hill behind us and there was a convenient little shop with a butcher nearby.

25 April. Left in the rain and it stayed with us all day and as usual once, you got to the locks it seemed to get heavier. The locks were all automated, but Charleville Mézieres was the difficult one, with the terrible mooring that we remembered the last time when we had Brandy on board with us; it had now been all rearranged and looked fantastic. Today we had moved into new territory and the scenery changed considerably with the Meuse having downsized to river size and changed its name to Canal de l'Est Branch Nord. However, we made a bad mistake not stopping at Sedan and going on to Mouzon where we found the mooring under construction and in the stream, so crash-landed and had no choice but to stay, it will be an exercise to leave in the morning.

26 April. Both the Captain (worrying about the departure) and the First Mate (worrying about strange noises with a background of loud music until 6AM) had a bad night. We departed by backing down stream, the wheel hard to starboard and the use of the bow prop, we made it, actually quite well, worried for nothing. It was still raining, cats and dogs; even though the locks worked smoothly, we were drenched. Still could appreciate the scenery, even in the rain, thinking how lovely it would have been in the sun. We moored up at Dun-sur-Meuse, lovely moorings (le relais de la Truite), water and electricity and it managed to stop raining for a few hours. We managed to get the TV rigged up and surprise it worked, also a couple of running repairs but we had a good night!

27 April. Maybe if we stop talking about the weather it might stop raining, but it did not and the scenery was obviously lovely but getting fed up with looking at it through the windscreen wipers; lots of birds and we saw a kingfisher. We passed nine locks but lock 24 (Consenvoye) was an experience in itself as it had sloping walls, luckily going up you could see them, would need attention going down. We moored up at Verdun, where they had new facilities with water and electricity, set between the bridges of Beaurepaire and Chausée.

28 April. Dare we say it NO RAIN and it managed to stay that way until we moored up at

Saint Mihiel. Went shopping and the heavens opened but the sun returned around 16:30 hours. Most of the trip today had been on the canal but we moved back onto the Meuse and the larger towns. Traces of the war remain in the form of military cemeteries. We had passed through another nine locks, but beginning to get a little concerned, as we have not found any fuel.

29 April. We awoke to fog and cold, the temperature had dived overnight. Left for the first lock of the day, wondering whether we should, we were out of the stream heading for the lock to find a barge 'stuck' in the entrance. Not stuck in fact it was being refueled, they eventually moved when they realised Deuxième Folie was there. The day continued without incident and we were gaining in experience. Unfortunately, we could not make use of that fuel, as it was the cheap fuel for barges and a different colour. The Meuse was very swollen and flowing over the top of the lock at Commercy, it was to be closed after us and the barge following, we were at the right time again. So we now had ten locks upstream, which made ten ladders, which the First Mate had to climb out of and help the lock keeper. The Captain did another tunnel and she was excellent, it was easier as they had upstream and downstream hours and it was well lit. We then entered into the Canal de la Marne-au-Rhin and into the twelve automated locks downstream; passing two barges and finally ending up in Toul where we had arranged to get fuel from a hire boat firm (Connoisseur Cruises). It was a long day but the sun was shining and that always helps.

30th April. After two locks and a bridge, we arrived at the Connoisseur Cruises base and got our fuel – at a price 150 litres 862.50 FF, i.e. 5.77FF per litre. After that, another lock and we entered the Moselle canalisé with three very large locks and approximately twenty-three kilometres of beautiful views, water and trees in the sun. We then turned into the Canal Est Branch Sud and flogged our way through seventeen manual locks. We moored up at Charmes eventually staying until Monday due to lock closures and fatigue. It was a lovely spot they had water, electricity and the TV was working, we certainly needed a rest, as we were really tired. We worked on the boat as usual correcting problems, mainly wet ones, which brings to mind the daily collection of 20FF mooring fees by two ladies and their umbrellas.

We both felt much better for the rest we had probably been pushing ourselves too much. We had a visit from an English couple who were with their boat 'Six Bells' and would follow us, but much later. We cycled around five kilometres to visit the Charmes Military Cemetery, Essesome (small with only 215 identified casualties), Captain was a little puffed, it was the First Mate who had been getting all the exercise with the ladders, but at least on the return it was downhill.

4th May. Unbelievably we have been on the water now for two weeks and now we have two days of heavy locks to look forward to, after that we should make speedier progress. We left at 09:00 hours on a very cold grey morning although later the sun came out, the sky was blue but it was very cold due to the wind. During the day, we touched the bottom once and the top of the red duster scraped a bridge, at 3.50 metres we had five cms to spare, but at the next bridge, the water had risen by 10 cms so we touched. We started the day with sixteen locks, just to name a few: Vincy, Portieux, Avière, La Heronnière, Vaxoncourt, and Thaon. We ended the day with a flight of sixteen locks with two lock keepers alternating we reached the Summit and moored up at 18:15 hours not bad going with only two barges going down interrupting us. Apparently, there are more following us but only three to pass on now, then finally we will be going down. The night was spent at Chaumousey, it had been a hard day again some thirty-five kilometres and thirty locks and the three left, left us in good standing for the morning.

5th May. We knew we had another hard day ahead of us and after the vidange we left around 09:30 hours We were alone in the first lock and then locked through the rest with a German Yacht, only two barges and two 'Locaboats' passing going upstream otherwise very quiet with the weather dry, sun in and out but very cold. At some point, there had been a problem with Lock 2 and the fire brigade had been called out, apparently kids throwing stones and blocking the door, pleased to say it was all clear by the time we got there, but we could hear the Bargee's moaning on the VHF. As anticipated, it was a long tiring day with thirty-four locks and over thirty kilometres but we arrived at Fontenoy-le-Château, which had full facilities.

6th May. The day started with the washing in the mooring facilities and it was raining although we had clean clothes we had wet clothes (no dryer available). We then fueled up (not having used as much as we thought) and moved off around noon. We then faced eleven automated locks and one manual at Corre and then we entered the Soâne. It stopped raining and we had 'flags' hanging outside trying to dry the washing and a line rigged up inside in the corridor. We then went through two more automatic locks (with poles now) and eventually stopped at Jussey (this ancient bastion came self-sufficient under the Duke of Burgundy and the Houses of Spain, afterwards under the Crown of France it was finally able to prosper in peace). We moored with two hire boats and as it was only a small jetty so one moored alongside us.

7th May. Lovely scenery and a lot more boats on the move, we went through one guard lock and then we were sent the long way round and that was lovely as we saw swans and more wild life, obviously going where the boats do not normally go. We had one tunnel (St. Albin 680 metres and one way at a time) and we were just coming out when another boat from the opposite end started to come in. He had to back out – lock keeper error and he admitted this to us. The evening was spent in a Port de Plaisance de Savoyeux, many boats, had a shower, hair wash and then walked to the village to shop. We had bought a special liquor/apero wine made from honey from the lock at Soing – excellent. The Captain can say that with all honesty we had SUN, I mean proper sun we sat on the deck for supper and all wet washing is now dry.

Reference in the log mentions the GPS, which seems not to be working a lot of the time; this was a farewell gift from Jacques' office gang, together with fun and serious lifesaving equipment!

One of the Safety Gifts

8th May. This day is still recognised in France because of the war and the shops only opened for a limited period. We started the day with another tunnel (tunnel de Savoyeux 643 metres). We seem to be making more progress now the number of locks are diminishing, lots of hire boats around with the incumbent amateurs, like sticking to the map when the actual signs do not exist and on crash course, the First Mate had to yell at them. We moored up for the night at Auxonne nice town beautiful Church and we will visit in the morning. Interesting historical point in June 1788, the Auxonne Garrison saw the arrival of a certain Lt. Bonaparte, then 18 years of age, he stayed until April 1791 when he left for Valence.

The man at the mooring chatting about hire boats informed us one had ended up on the weir!

9th May. The Soâne continues to amaze us by its size, probably up to one hundred and fifty kilometres wide in places. Of course, the sun shining helps making it another beautiful day, the number of pleasure boats was down again until we moored up, even so we could imagine in full season it must be packed, interestingly we passed one American and one Canadian boat. Refueled at St. Jean-de-Losne (which was also the junction to the Canal de Bourgogne) at a proper place at a proper price 4.50FF; also changed the gas bottle – no Esso in France so had to pay for vidange to Butagax also 210FF. Now at Chalon-sur-Soâne, 105FF per night but 165FF for two, so we decided to take Sunday off and stay for two nights.

10th May. Having decided to have a 'rest day' we relaxed in the sun wrote a lot of postcards and washed Deuxième Folie. The American's moored up (l'Amité) and they knew Chuck

Wilson from SHAPE, small world. It was market day so went into town back to the boat and then back to the town again later to take photos, again lost over the years.

11ᵗʰ May. We made a 08:00 hours start and moored at 18:00 hours and we finally agreed for the first time ever that the Soâne was getting boring, suffice it to say we just continued, the scenery was always the same, very rare you saw anything interesting. A couple of pleasure boats passed – one Brit going like a bat out of hell (Lady Monaco). We moored at Yachting 69 near Neuville-sur-Saône alongside the Santa Maria, with only two locks and the downstream it allowed us to cover long distances, without pushing.

12ᵗʰ May. We then moved on and passed Lyon, which was interesting but not spectacular but it was with great pleasure that we then left the Saône and onto the Rhone, the scenery changed everything, the vines were beginning to appear on the hillsides and of course the sun was brilliant. We were now suffering from sunburn instead of webbed feet. We passed two (Pierre Bénite & Vaugris) of the thirteen locks on the Rhone, BIG – 195m long and 12m wide. Moored up at Les Roches-de-Condrieu, pretty little marina, small village but essentials available (obviously wine!). Interesting bit of history in that the town is famous for its 'bargeeters' this is where the 'cul de piau', bargee's who navigated the Rhone were recruited from.

13ᵗʰ May. We took a leisurely start at 09:45 hours and it was another beautiful day, only one dull patch through an industrial area but otherwise the scenery remained lovely and another three locks (Sablons, Gervans & Bourg-les-Valence). Moored up backwards, always a feat with Deuxième Folie in the Port de l'Epervière at Valence. Boaters would come back from the Mediterranean to this port to spend the winter, quite an undertaking given the Rhone stream and the lack of facilities on the way up. No existing proof but the Captain sat on the top deck 'topless' getting her tan up to speed, waving to anyone around all totally unknown – she hoped.

14ᵗʰ May. This proved to be a heavy day even though we set off at 08:30 hours did not moor up until 19:45 hours. Not that there were many locks but we lost a lot of time at four (Beauchastel, Châteauneuf, Bollène & Caderousse) of the five and the last one taking one and a half hours. Today we passed our deepest yet twenty-three metres deep, at least it was cool down at the bottom, the day had been hot, no wind even when the boat was moving. We moored up at Port 2, which was in a small bay off the rigours of the fast flowing current of the Rhone and much appreciated as it had all facilities including a good restaurant.

15ᵗʰ May. We had a short day, after yesterday, just to Avignon only twenty-eight kilometres and one lock. Lovely town of 'Sur-le-Pont d'Avignon' fame very touristic, moorings good but difficult (backwards again) because of the wind and current also having to go against the current to refuel was difficult. Therefore, any thoughts of us trying to go back up the Rhone were rapidly disappearing.

16ᵗʰ May. Well we finally got to the end of the Rhone, passing Tarascon and Arles (famous for its Amphitheatre) then on to the Petit Rhone and then the Canal du Rhone à Sete, whilst this is canalised, it runs parallel with the Mediterranean and was very impressive. Whilst uneventful, the canal finally produced 'people' fishing, there were flowers on the edge of the canal, and we moored up in the wilds but we took the bikes to the Camargue Plaisance for shopping.

17ᵗʰ May. Sunday and we really enjoyed the trip. We did a stop at Aigues-Mortes having taken the detour to find it when we did we could not lock the door on the boat. Something had got into the lock, so it was taken out and soaked in Acetone, blocked the door with wood and finally visited Aigues-Mortes – why did we bother – it was another tourist trap. On the way, again we passed all the Etangs and could finally see the Mediterranean in the distance. We had heard there was a problem at Frontignan – it was still there 'Pont on Panne', when we arrived with a possible delay of seven days or go to sea. After chatting to neighbours (after the Captain had made a fantastic mooring) and they were expecting a pilot to take them – the dye was set! We had an evening out at the 'Bonne Bouffe' with a surprised Marie-Claude who was the ex-wife of Jean-Claude Menuet (old colleague from NATO).

18ᵗʰ May. The day to remember we went to sea NEVER AGAIN, the Captain panicked – it was basically terrifying, the TV/Satellite crashed to the floor and bottles and oil in the galley – put it down to experience but although she can cope with waves Deuxième Folie did not have enough ballast to cope with the swell which was something else. The First Mate did the steering and looked as though we were heading out to sea and no sign of the entry to the Port, but he did find it. The port was interesting with five bridges opening on specified times. Lost the Red Duster – not a bridge too far but a bridge too low – recovered it and it is now shorter. Finally, we entered the Etang de Thau, calm and without problems, the First Mate plotted the route with the GPS and we steered with the compass and memories of problems finding the entrance to the Canal du Midi eighteen years ago faded into oblivion, but not the oysters even though we did not stop this time. Good news the round lock at Adge was now automated so no problems. We moored at Villeneuve-les-Beziers, at the halt nautique 'les Berges au canal'.

19ᵗʰ May. Glorious day really feeling as though we are home now that we are on the Canal du Midi again. So many new things, which is not surprising after eighteen years. We started at 08:00 hours with an elderly couple who were worse than unless in the lock. Poor lock keepers. Held up at Ecluse de l'Orb, the two lock features had been redone into one large one with sliding poles, originally Bezièr and l'Orb locks, followed by crossing the Orb via the 240m long aqueduct.

Aqueduct

Then up the Foncérannes flight – fantastic – what else can we say finally in our own boat and in the sun.

Foncérannes

Saw several Red Dusters – got the naval salute from one obviously very patriotic British lady. We passed one small tunnel 'Percée de Malpas' single passage, just beside the Oppidum d'Ensérune. Capestang lovely corner and Poilhes with a lovely looking restaurant beside the Canal called l'Auberge de la Croisade. We passed the junction for Port-la-Nouvelle (Canal de la Robine) and arrived at Ventenac en Minervois and found Tony and Therèsa at their restaurant 'Le Coustelous' where we had supper together with Jacques and Brigitte having found them without problems and they made us so welcome. We filled up with the local wine at local prices from the Chateau that that Jacques and Brigitte had initiated us on how to do so.

20th May. We eventually made a 12:40 hours departure after Aperitif at Tony & Theresa's, they gave us some magret de canard to take with us for the evening BBQ, as well as bread as the baker would be shut on Wednesday. Except for tourists (who are indescribable), the trip was uneventful. One single lock (Argens - with lady lock keeper), where six Germans managed to get into the lock without being able to hang onto anything. First Mate ended up climbing out via the ladder on the lock door, knight to the rescue, fixed them and then us and he was awarded with two German beers! Two doubles, two single locks and a final double mooring up for the night at Puichéric followed this exercise.

21st May. With our 08:00 hours departure, we progressed well through three doubles, one triple and one single lock at Marseillette. A German in a small sailing boat caused havoc at the Trèbes triple lock, went across the entrance and then said you go first by which time he had then managed to get in and left us hardly any room – amateurs – we managed to lose him at lunch. Still very much at home on this Canal and everything still looks beautiful. Moored up in the countryside near Carcassonne in full sun watching it set.

22nd May. Long hard day, met interesting people, made water alongside a couple of youngsters who were arranging an old barge (Bec du Boule) but as they were putting in 2,000 litres it cost one hour and then before we knew it was lunchtime and the lock keeper took one hour twenty minutes. Captain not well but struggled on. Had one boat with us with eight on board and were useless so we ended up rushing round to sort them out! They were much more organised by the time we left them, French this time as opposed to German. The day had been composed of fourteen single, two doubles, one triple and one quadruple lock, taking us to Castelnaudary where we spent the evening.

23rd May. The Captain was still very much under the weather (bronchitis as usual) but carried on as any good Wren would. The trip started with two single locks (La Domergue & Laplanque), one triple (Laurens), one double (Du Roc) and finally the last one 'Mediterranée' we had reached the top of the Canal du Midi and arrived at Le Ségala, Deuxième Folie's new permanent mooring.

Ségala

<u>**TOTAL TRIP**</u>: 1,582 Kilometres, 707 Locks, 7 Bridges and 4 Tunnels.

CHAPTER SEVEN – STRANGE TIMES

The boat life took on a different aspect now having got her to her new home mooring and we then had to return to Belgium for the big move to happen.

We left 'La Folie' ahead of the removal van with the three Labradors, who really do not like the car. The dog barrier had been installed in the Renault Espace and the dogs had been given their tranquilisers – ha ha – ten minutes down the road and they had managed to dismantle the dog barrier and cause havoc regardless of the tranquilisers. We stopped, looked at each other and gave them another pill each, we then tried to reattach the barrier, easier said than done, but decided instead of the gentle drive down with overnight stop it would have to be done in one go. The dogs were by now completely out for the count, when we stopped to let them pee they staggered around the parking lot and had to be lifted back into the car. Glad to say we made it without further incident but it was a long drive from Belgium to Castelnaudary.

The dogs were disorientated to say the least but took to the old settee reluctantly (theirs was in the removal van) and we all slept. It was probably about three days later the movers arrived and thankfully, the first item off was their settee and the three of them leapt on it in great relief. By now all the second hand furniture we had in the house and been given away and we set about settling all our items from Belgium and finding places for everything. The removers were excellent, everything done and they were going to sleep in the van outside, before returning to Belgium We offered them a swim plus we did a BBQ and a good evening was had by all and they were rested for their return trip to Belgium the next day.

At some point later, the dogs tried to walk on water! the pool had a blue bubble cover and of course, one tried it, Jacques rushed to wind it in, then another one went in on the other-side. Brandy on the other hand just watched still remembering her incident in the lock obviously. Therefore, we eventually got them out via the steps and in hindsight; it was a 'good' accident as the three of them refused to go anywhere near the pool again!

We settled in, got the house in good shape, Deuxième Folie was not neglected, and she was worked on convenient moored outside the local café Relais de Riquet. However, it would be the year 2000 before we started with trips again, with visitors, in between she had been used as extra accommodation for extra visitors, regardless that we had four bedrooms at the house. France ended up being a free hotel for many over the years; and it was an easy drive for everyone to come by car!

Sue decided she wanted to organise something and launched the Fête de la Musique au Sommet du Canal and this ran for five years and Deuxième Folie was used as an art gallery at one point, also moved to help hang the banner over the bridge.

Fète de la Musique au Sommet du Canal (FMSC)

She had to be moved during December and January to deeper water, which we did together with Jill & Tony and their narrow boat to Négra, due to the emptying of the canal for planned works on locks, diminishing mud build-ups etc.

Winter Closure

It was not until **2000** that we made a seven-day trip. The first day was **Sunday 16th July**, Luc, Nathalie and Max joined, and we made a record trip to Castelnaudary in three hours with all the locks in our favour. Filled up with gas oil and toured the Basin and then Luc, Nathalie and Max went home (we think Jill & Tony must have collected them) because we stayed the night.

Well on the **17th July** we were punished for the easy day before – the battery was dead. Therefore, after getting the generator and then the boat up and running we were good to go, however, after a stop for lunch, we had a repeat performance with the generator and this would have to be a daily chore until such time we were able to buy a new battery. We spent the night at Sauzens, which was a good mooring, but it was 19:15 hours when we stopped, so a little tired.

The **18th July** we faced our first real traffic jam at Trébes – three hours and this is likely to continue tomorrow, there are so many hire boats on the go. First big sailing error we got hitched on the side in a lock bang went the new woodwork, it sounded worse than it was, but repair will be necessary. Still with the battery problems and now a fuse for some of the lights had blown, happy days. Due to hold ups, it was again a late mooring at 20:15 hours near Marseillette.

Set off on the morning of **19th July** and entered the first lock at Marseillette and the backlog had gone and we were straight in. Next followed the triple (Ecluse Fonfile) and then we were back to the waiting again for the double (Ecluse St. Martin), two kilometres and into the next double (l'Aiguille) another three kilometres and into another double (Puichéric) then a single and passing Homps (very busy area due to a boat hiring outlet). Next was a double (Pechlaurier) followed by Argens which was the last before making our objective of Le Somail for the night where we had a superb meal at the Auberge Lou Somaillon, which had an excellent site on the edge of the Canal du Midi. The fuses we thought were blown were now working but the boat was badly in need of a service, as the bow prop had also not been working.

Le Somail

Next morning **20th July,** we left around 09:00 hours, already turning back but unfortunately, a large barge was ahead. We stopped at Ventenac and met up with Jacques and Brigitte (mentioned already above who were old friends from Belgium and had also performed at the Fête de la Musique) they brought us bread, the First Mate stocked up on wine at the Chateau the only thing missing was the Boursin. We then passed the barge mentioned above to find it had stopped at Homps so we continued and stopped at La Redorte, shopped and had a beer and filled with water. We then passed back through the locks mentioned above eventually mooring at 20:00 hours at Puichéric – next problem gas alarm would not stop, First Mate bypassed the alarm to solve it and we ate very late!

Early start on the **21st July**, into the first lock at 08:15 hours trying to get ahead by starting early due to the heat of yesterday. A few bangs and bumps at locks and bridges, roll on the bow prop being mended. Lunched under the trees at Trébes after passing this triple lock another four kilometres to Ecluse Villedubert, followed by L'évêque, another three kilometres to the Fresquel with its lock, basin, followed by a double. Then two more singles and back to Carcassonne, then followed two more singles, one double and we finally moored up again at Sauzens around 18:30 hours.

Saturday **22nd July** we faced the long trip home, starting at 08:15 hours and reaching Ségala at 19:45. High winds, difficult trip, fenders burst, First Mate in the drink (he missed the bank). Captain decided that she would not go out again until everything was in working order!

TOTAL TRIP: 219 KMs and 117 Locks

Two small trips followed one on the 8th August just one lock to Port-de-Lauragais with the First Mate in Charge, together will Jean-Philippe plus family and Amandine, the second done by the Captain with the winners of the Tombola, Baptiste and Aurelie, plus others.

NEW DIRECTION

Finally, on our own, except for Brandy on **15th August** we took the direction towards the Atlantic, well what a pleasant surprise from the other side green and interesting. Not a lot of traffic and the trip was smooth – the bow prop was still working. We started with Ecluse Océan (No. 17) instead of heading for the Mediterranean; we were now heading towards the Ocean. There was a single lock (Emborrel) then a double (Encassan), two singles, Renneville and Gardouch where we ended up having lunch at 12:15 hours and finally moored up in a super spot at PK19, which was approximately half way between Donneville and St. Jouzy Brandy nearly ended up in the drink again but bottom only this time. We had passed Laval, Negra, Sanglier (which was a double), Aygvesvives, and Mongiscard to get there.

The **16th August** was a day that could have been organised better! We arrived at Port Sud Toulouse around 11:30 hours, no opening until 14:00 hours and prior to that we had lost forty-five minutes at the first lock waiting for two yachts. Patrick (Jacques' oldest son) arrived with First Mate's pills; we had a beer, lunch generally passing the time. About 13:40 hours the Captain wanders over and re-reads opening hours and it was not 14:00 but 16:00. Therefore, we left and we still have not put gas oil in the boat. We were now back into a series of perches again, problem at the first, green light not working, so missed one tour. Finally turned into the Canal lateral à la Garonne, the first Ecluse was La Lande, followed by Lacourtensourt and Fenouillet, lovely but no moorings and the train was alongside. We finally moored at Ecluse Lespinasse ready for the morning, lovely evening/night: thunderstorm, trains and Brandy who does not like thunderstorms!

The voyage continued on the **17th August**, the trip was smooth, and we entered into a more touristic area after we had passed the silos a good job we moored where we did. There were another six locks and approximately eighteen kilometres and we then arrived at the water slope at Montech, unfortunately not for tourists and we had to pass along side via the five automated locks. We stopped at 16:30 hours in Castelsarrasin, lovely moorings and a place where the boat could be left. Had supper out and Brandy behaved beautifully, however, another storm so another bad night.

Well **18th August** turned out to be a horrendous day, the bow got stuck in one the lock doors and it was automatic, we were hoping the glass fibre would hold up and not break, finally loud cracking of wood and the front gave way. Damage quite small compared with the horrendous noise and sound effects. Captain a quaking heap. Other than that, we had made our intended destination after twelve locks and twenty-five kilometres, which turned out to be a 'dirty hole' Valence d'Agen. It only took two minutes to decide to go back to Moissac (another five locks and seventeen kilometres) and it was on that return we had the problem with the automated lock mentioned above. Spent the night at Moissac (40FF) hoped for fuel but pump empty and as it was 6.70 per litre, we would not have filled up anyway. A pleasant town, a tunnel type exit via a swing bridge.

We stayed at Moissac the morning of the **19th August** leaving at 13:30 hours and arriving at Castelsarrasin at 16:00 hours on the Saturday. Back to the nice free moorings, really lovely spot and we decided to stay there and relax until Monday morning. Sunday was a lovely day and we ended up having a drink with the Mayor on the opening of Capitanerie with their staff Sylvie and Rebecca. We lunched at the restaurant Deux Ponts – very good and the evening entertainment with Los Grillos, a Jazz Group, was really good except Brandy had a hissy fit at the end of the evening, she probably thought the loud music was thunder again!

In line with our planning, we left on Monday the **21st August** and headed for Montech, first taste of rain enroute but moored up before the heavy rain hit after passing the five automated locks. Walked to Intermarché, Gas oil (20L jerry can), bow prop still working, Montech was a busy halt (40FF) but as an early start in the morning was intended, we had a relaxing evening on board.

We left at 08:00 hours on **22nd August** knowing it was going to be a long day. The Dutch had left at 07:45 hours thus the first lock was closed and so it continued but with luck, we cleared the last manual one at 12:25 hours and did not have to wait for the one-hour lunch break. Noises from the boat enroute and we finally stopped and the filter was blocked, our fault with the dirty water we had been through we should have checked. We were now back on the Canal du Midi and took photos of the rather impressive graffiti on the way into Toulouse – again lost pictures. The large lock caused a few problems we were too long for one rope and too short for two. The First Mate held the front rope and the Captain held the boat on the engine but they brought us up slowly so no problems. We arrived at Port Sud and finally got gas oil, 300 litres at a cost of 2,000FF and it was where we moored for the night.

The **23rd August** was a pleasant easy morning with lunch in Port Sud leaving around 13:30 hours, at the first lock we were three together for the trip, locks quite deep First Mate had to climb out with the ropes. These locks were a pain as they had leaking walls, i.e. peeing out of holes in the wall and soaked the boat. Passed the Dutch at Montgiscard and we moored up at Ayguesvives for the night, very pleasant spot. The nearby restaurant was closed and the other was a five KM walk, we decided to BBQ instead - excellent.

Took off late on **24th August** around 10:30 hours took our time passing Gardouch just before lunch. Stopped at Renneville (wine and cheese – after large breakfast). No problems idling for passenger boat and we met Robert (owner of the passenger boat) again at the l'Ocean lock, with South Africans. Phoned Patrick and they were watching from the balcony and picked us up at Ségala.

TOTALTRIP 240KMs and 95 locks.

CHAPTER EIGHT – 2001/2002

The year has as usual been busy with visitors and short trips out with them; the usual one was down to Castelnaudary, a visit to the market, a chicken from the spit and picnic on the banks. So easy to 'park' with a boat on market day with the car it is not so easy. Also took our American friends who live at the old lock keepers house at the Ecluse Ocean.

Sally & David Pabst – US Friends

September 1st saw us set off for a trip on our own except for Brandy, with Jill & Tony at home with the other two dogs plus their dog Charlie (long haired dash hound who loved to swim!), also thanks to Tony for the screwdriver, cannot remember what for anymore. We phoned our US friends that live in the lock keepers cottage at l'Ocean lock and they said the lock was ready so off we were at 11:30 hours. We had a 'puddle jumper' for company in that lock but afterwards we were on our own, passing again Renneville, Négra, Ayguesvives and St. Jouzy Uneventful first day and we moored up at the same place as last year at PK19.

Ready at 08:00 hours on the **2nd September** and lock keeper was fifteen minutes late, not that it was important since vandals had attacked the lock in Toulouse and managed to empty a bief. So we had a one hour delay at Matabiau crawled out eventually at a 'dead slow and stop speed' with only forty centimetres under us at times. Thus, it continued until the last automated lock – which did not automate, so another wait to be helped by VNF (Voies Navigables de France). We really pushed then joining again the Canal Lateral à la Garonne, having passed some ten locks and done forty-two kilometres but managed to make Montech where the mooring was still 40FF per night.

Departed on the **3rd September** at a reasonable hour of 10:00 hours and the lock 'ladies' were ready for us to pass the five automated locks by-passing the slope. We could have taken the slope this year but at a price 230FF per person plus another night's wait, we decided we could live without it for 500FF and spend that on good food and wine. So passed the five automated locks and the following three manual ones, although the last bief was down to thirty centimetres in places. Moored up at Castelsarrasin, lovely as usual and only 10FF per night all in. Will seriously think of putting her here for winter if they empty Ségala again at a cost of 700FF for three months guarded by the resident Capitainerie. As it was so nice we spent another night, did a little sanding on the woodwork and the clowns look happy – we had taken off the 'hippocamps' on the outside of the boat and replaced them with happy clowns (produced by Luc & Patrick), much more our style.

Eventually on the **5th September** got Marraine on the phone to wish her happy birthday and a call to the boys to remind them! Left as planned but we were hampered by a Peniche (sightseeing boat) – he even pissed off the lock keeper. Lost more time than planned – had lunch in a lock and decided to stop at Moissac. Met two Brits with sailboats 'Solitaire' and 'Seqonia', we gave them some info and it will be interesting to see if they stopped at Ségala. A few problems at Pont du Tarn with wind and current but the Captain recovered. No diesel – vandals – but still only 10FF for the night at Moissac.

We left at 10:00 hours on **6th September** as agreed so that we could pass the swing bridge, a very smooth day, we were alone, but depth was not good and many weeds, so only known stops were reliable. We put 130 litres in at Agen, unfortunately at Locaboat prices; we wondered who the vandals were as after Port Sud (Toulouse) then Agen it was the first possible place to refill. We had faced different auto lock systems and we had to reopen the doors but eventually got the hang of it. Moored up on the bank using our spikes, lovely spot but now really in unknown territory, Valence d'Agen had not improved.

The **7th September** turned out to be one of those days, after the day before's smooth one, malfunction of automatic locks, Captain hit a couple of locks, First Mate did not watch the woodwork and we blew up one fender and that was on coffee (i.e. not wine), maybe that was the problem; weather also 'iffy' but cleared up. Although we started at 09:35 hours, we did not moor up until 18:10 hours. Met Andre (Mirabelle) who screamed a big welcome to us to stop – so another unplanned stop with an amusing sortie of Brandy with the use of towels. Met a couple of Brits who lived nearby and had seen the Red Duster.

We continued with four locks in quick succession (Agen, Mariannettes, Chabrières and Rosette) another fifteen kilometres and a small lock, Ecluse l'Auvignon (only 1,03 metres deep). Another seven kilometres brought us to a double (Baïse and Larderet), passing the town of Buzet-sur-Baïse; another nine kilometres to the Ecluse Berry then five to Ecluse La Gaulle then three kilometres to Ecluse La Gaulette after another three kilometres we arrived to spend the night at 'Lagruère' Halt and had supper (50FF each!) but it was good.

The **8th September** was a nothing special day and we thought some of the long stretches were a little boring but we made our intended destination the lock prior to the river and the sea 'Castets-en-Dorthe' and ate at the small restaurant at the Capitainerie which had been recommended by friends. The last lock was four metres automated but manned also; it rained heavily during the night.

Off we were on **9th September** at 09:00 hours we turned back as we certainly had no intention of going to sea; it had stopped raining but we did not stop until 18:30 hours one of those long days – too long, but we had promised André (who made us stop earlier) we would return to Buzet-sur-Baïse for supper. We lost a good forty-five minutes at one lock to find out one boat had turned the perche after exiting so he could make a little trip and the lock would be ready on return. He had handicapped kids on board so I suppose … but not really on. We got stuck coming up, another bit of wood loose and some screwing enroute. Had a nice supper with André but it was outside and very damp, so Captain returned to the boat as the coughing was back and with it probably the usual bronchitis! We stayed another night at Buzet, borrowed André's car and did some shopping, weather still good but Captain still coughing.

11th September 2001, this was to turn out to be a memorable day, it was the Captain's birthday also. We started at 10:25 hours with a smooth run and no problems with the four locks before Agen; in fact, they were completed in fifty minutes. The area we thought looked boring on the way down looked much better in the sun. We moored up at the Halte Nautique de Boé, closed already for the winter but in the countryside and very quiet. We received a phone call from Dottie for happy birthday wishes and that was how we learned something terrible had happened in the US. We tried to get radio or something to work, tried to ask the neighbours and they were not very friendly. So we walked up to the supermarket and watched the TV, everyone was in shock about the attacks on the twin towers; we would have to wait until we are home to hear more.

The intended trip to 'la Baise' and The Lot had to be missed, as we were too wide for two of the Locks, thank goodness we found out in time.

The **12th September** was a long day as we knew it would be although leaving at 09:00 hours we did not moor up at Castelsarrasin until 18:30 hours where we intended to stay for a couple of days. The weather remains good and we had no real problems we passed our 'bogie' lock where there were three on duty one being in the water with a rowing boat. He took a ride up the lock hanging on the back of us, the lock keepers really worked with us enabling us to make our destination having done sixteen locks and forty-five kilometres. As mentioned above we stayed here for a couple of days as intended and we needed to relax.

Started again on **15th September** as anticipated with one yacht waiting for us at the first lock, not very handy, we had to wait for them at Montech, but only for about ten minutes, we had already decided not to take the branch to Montauban, we then moored up after the lock as planned very calm and a good idea. So a relatively short day for us only six locks and fourteen kilometres.

We departed on **16th September** at 09:00 hours knowing we had fifteen kilometres without locks then into the dirty area, which we got through prior to lunch break. Lost and recovered one fender, wind bad in places, the large lock in Toulouse a doddle ONE ROPE NO HANDS. Met up with Stan and Pat Schaub with their boat 'Easy Street' (very old NADGEMO colleagues) exchanged coordinates after a good chat. Lovely ride through Toulouse and eventually moored up just after Port Sud in the countryside and happy to be back on the Canal du Midi.

17th September started being alone in the calm, then one boat leaped ahead of us but the lock keeper had seen him and he had to wait for us; then held up at the double due to two coming downstream, thus a forced stop at Négra for lunch. We passed a couple of 'new boaters' thinking they were stopping, then they started again and stayed with us to l'Ocean where Sally & Dave (our American friends) were waiting for us. Stopped for a drink and then headed to Ségala and home.

TOTAL TRIP: 487 KMs and 135 Locks.

2002

Again, most of the year was spent running visitors and family on short trips including an old school friend Wendy & Bernard (Merrien), who also now live in France.

The only trip made was a Boy Scout mission to help Dominique who had broken down the other side of Carcassonne. Therefore, we had a madcap rush to load Deuxième Folie and get Jill & Tony to look after the dogs and the house, and off we were at 09:00 hours on **5th October**, smooth start until the triple where we had to wait forty-five minutes for an ancient pusher moving at approximately one kilometre per hour! So lunch in Castelnaudary and onwards, chaos at Bram with all the hire boats and the Canadians filling up with water. Managed to make it to the top of Béteille for the night (19:00 hours), weather good, had supper and early night 10PM!

On the **6th October** we were through the first lock at 09:00 hours with the Canadians, sun very bright and difficult to see, the Canadians ended up in the bank we continued and managed to lose them at the next lock. We made Carcassonne by 12:30 hours, met by Dominique. His boat is another five locks down-stream under the triple he had no engine and no rudder! Arrived tied him up behind and the great rescue started, it was like having a caravan behind you that was jack-knifing. Unbelievably we made it to the VNF yard (in Carcassonne) in two and a half hours, with a very relieved Dominique and Deuxième Folie who was none the worse for wear. Lock keepers were fantastic and we all sat enjoying a well-earned drink together with some Swiss moored up beside us. We ate out in a suspect Italian restaurant and Sauzens was still a good stop for a water top-up on the way back.

The **7ᵗʰ October** was the day to return home and after a shower in the VNF facilities (still bad leak on Deuxième Folie), a really smooth trip and we made it as far as St. Roch 12:45 hours enroute for the Mediterranean and stopped for lunch at the new moorings delaying the last stretch as long as possible. The Boy Scout exercise ended up with a total of 116 KMs and 72 locks!

CHAPTER NINE – 2003

We had the usual mini-trips with visitors and it was not until September that we were able to take time for ourselves, so much for retirement!

We left, together with faithful Brandy, on the **6th September** around 09:00 hours in the sun, unfortunately new rules had been put in force either you pass the lock on the hour or with a full lock – i.e. more than one boat. Interprétation! Filled up at Castelnaudary (150FF) and arrived two minutes late for four locks at St. Roch, so that was where we spent the night and guess what - shower does not work – First Mate will have to work. The second day passed, rain and more rain and rules and full locks and amateurs, including the jumping Belge, Americans who knew nothing and of course the Brits – not a lot to add to that. We were, of course, on familiar territory already mentioned before. Moored up at Marseillette, First Mate still thinking about shower, hope we are not smelling yet! I often wondered why we pushed so much we were crazy, sixty-two kilometres and thirty-four locks.

Usual problems on the **8th September** as above with bumper boats – Brits again. Did a crossover in the Foncérannes and got a thumbs-up from the lock keeper and Captain had a dodgy bow-prop, it worked more off than on. Moored up at Ventenac on the 54 KM stretch without locks and ate at the 'old Tony' restaurant the Pasta was very good, chatted to the new owner and went to bed at 10PM, just as well as we had a terrible night chicks going mad at 2AM and the wine pickers (with their noisy machines) started at 5AM.

9th September as intended was a short day only five kilometres to the Le Somail and a very lazy day just as well after last night. Jacques and Brigitte arrived lunchtime for drinks, we had stocked up on wine as usual in Ventenac. Thus, we spent the nights of 9th and 10th September at Le Somail where the First Mate got the shower working, ha ha, just enough for two and back to square one. Bow-prop sorted, which required dismantling of the bed, extra lights working, little by little we were getting organised. Winds continued to be troublesome and a couple of boats 'bumped us' even though we were moored. We ate out and Brandy was welcome and good as usual, Captain was looking for non-existent shops, obviously the wrong village. Brandy happy as she has biscuits, it was the humans that had the problem. Ran the motor for hot water and as you can guess the shower went again.

The **11th September** and the Captain's birthday again being spent on Deuxième Folie, it was a quiet day although First Mate ended up in the water helping someone else, whilst the Captain took Brandy for a walk. We stopped at Poilhes (by passing Capestang) on the way, nearly a dead village but saw an art exhibition. Passed the Malpas tunnel and arrived at Colombier nice new port with all facilities, we had to moor outside due to the fact you had to back in and we could not get Brandy off the boat. Had an excellent supper out.

We left at 09:40 hours on the **12ᵗʰ September** enroute for the Bezier flight and met up with Jean-Louis and Beatrice (Nathalie's parents) who joined us for the lock experience but we had to wait three hours for the 13:30 hours off, Captain got thumbs-up from the lock keeper for the second time, at Foncérannes these ex-Wren's! After dropping off our guests after the aqueduct over the River Orb, we eventually moored up in the countryside near PK214, but due to the wind, the planned BBQ had to wait for another day.

We were now approaching with anticipation the crossing of the Etang de Thau so left at 09:15 hours on the **13ᵗʰ September**. We made the round lock at Adge and we were in prime position – we went, by accident, to the head of the queue. We had to wait for a pleasure boat but then it was our turn and we had made the Etang de Thau. We had a terrible job to find the entrance to the Canal and it was thanks to several fishermen we found it – but due to that delay, (it took us two and a half hours to cross), we missed the 17:00 hours for the Frontignan Bridge, so no choice night with trains and up for 09:00 hours. We were now on the Canal de Rhône à Sete.

Therefore, the **14ᵗʰ September** saw us up bright and early to 'catch' the bridge at 09:00 hours, even after a disturbed night with trains, cars, local party etc. All went well as we continued on the Canal and found it different, but a five-year interval is quite long, passing the Frontignan Bridge that had caused us to go to sea, reported on above. We tanked up on water at Palavas – quite an exercise – saw some interesting moorings but continued on to Aigues Mortes – mistake – no moorings available so we returned to the interesting ones we saw whilst making water at Palaras. Students warned us they were intending to have a party that evening but we heard nothing.

We decided to stay in our interesting moorings and move on to Latte tomorrow. The students got up around noon and the boat staggered off, we have now seen four large barges, like old times. First Mate tried to save one boatload; they finally moored up with the remaining member swimming across the canal to rejoin the boat. Said we would email photos, not sure, if we ever did. Captain was cleaning, windows of course, and First Mate doing odd jobs, the boat is slowly coming alive and it feels great.

Moved from our quiet mooring and saw the first large barges including one from Belgium. Stopped at Palavas showered and then entered Le Lez. Felt a little African Queenish on a river but very pleasant, one lock (Mirador) and then entered (just) into Port Ariane which was in fact a beautiful marina. Met some Brits (Maurine & Bob with their boat called the Grand Cru), supper with Laurent & Eliane Mistral old NATO friends. Then shopping, purchase of new battery, which will hopefully get the bow prop, working again, the Mistrals must remember us forever for purchasing batteries.

The **17ᵗʰ September** saw us having lunchtime drinks and snacks on Grand Cru, prior to that we had walked to the shops, did the Lotto, bought a UK paper today's really like a little village around the Marina. We set off with a working bow prop; it had been the battery, passed the lock at 14:30 hours and moored up as intended by the swing bridge. Had supper on the Peniche/Restaurant, very good and in excellent condition. Very relaxed day with only seven kilometres and the Mirador lock again.

Left on the **18th September** to the open swing bridge in a timely manner to shop and wait the opening of the Frontignan Bridge, map wrong again as it was 13:30 hours, which meant we had to leave our good mooring because of a Peniche. All went well, including the return across the Etang de Thau and we stopped at Marseillan, but we decided to continue, as the moorings were not readily available. We passed the first lock (Ecluse Bagnas) and moored up on the Herault, very pleasant except for the mosquitos.

The **19th September** saw us move from the moorings leaving, hopefully, the mosquitos behind. We passed the Round Lock alone and it was open and ready, we then went on to fill water tanks at Vias, someone in front as usual, but we managed although it took a lot of time. We also filled up on gas oil at Port Cassafières, a hire base so it was the usual higher price. We continued leaving the next night stop as flexible and passed the two locks prior to Foncérannes at 17:30 hours thinking that was it, but closing time now 18:00 hours and went up that magnificent flight on our own in thirty minutes it must have been a record especially with all the crowds watching us. We then decided to stop at our island in Colombier, small filter problem, rectified, no problems with the Malpas tunnel but late mooring up at 19:30 hours.

We left Colombier on **20th September** after an oil change and moved slowly forward, stopped at Poilhes for lunch – astronomical prices for water and electricity 2€ for 30 litres and 2€ for 45 minutes of electricity – no wonder no one uses it. We then carried on to spend the night in the countryside again, lovely BBQ bought from a good butcher in Colombier. Tomorrow we were ready to start our new experience.

On the **21st September,** we left at 10:00 hours and enthusiastically turned into the Canal de Junction, which was just before le Somail, but Captain hit mooring and plank fell off. Out with generator, drill and a quick fix. The locks here were automatic but very slow and closed for lunch and we had very eager Germans with us. We crossed the Aude, seemed much less important that the maps said and continued towards Narbonne, now on the Canal de la Robine – no moorings, thought we had found one but 'André' told us it was reserved, flogged on and it seemed endless finally mooring up before the Ecluse Mandirac at PK 18. The cruising through Narbonne under houses was impressive we hoped we would have better luck on the return in finding moorings.

The next morning on **22nd September** started with mozzie zapping 1cm from tummy button. We continued down for about one hour and then turned back: it was boring, humid and swarms of mozzies. We got back into Narbonne in time for the automated lock at 12 noon – one red light – early lunch for the lock keeper? - we finally passed at 14:15 hours after a phone call, we were now locked with two Germans at the next lock, then another, and so we were four. 'Luna' with the young Germans ahead we slowed down just before the Aude to allow two up-stream traffic to pass, then by the time we got to the first automated lock the young Germans had jumped in and started the system. Half an hour later we got in and then came the storm heavy rain, thunder and we stopped immediately after exiting where three others had also stopped. Brandy then decided to jump ship, First Mate got her, but as doors and windows had been open, we were wet inside and outside.

Surprisingly in the morning of **23rd September**, we had sun after one of the worst storms I think we have ever experienced with the boat. Although starting at 09:00 hours very slow morning, problems with the first lock due to the storm and a lock keeper was required. Slow progress continued with slow Brits and ever-slower Americans and it was 12 noon when we rejoined the Canal du Midi after passing the Canal de Junction. Well, joint consensus, we had done the Narbonne bit and will not bother again not worth the effort for twenty-four locks and thirty kilometres. Went back about eight kilometres to join Jill & Tony (Keogan) on their boat BuThubb'd (which means perfect in Bedouin) intending to have lunch but the restaurant was closed, so we snacked and then continued on to Ventenac, had supper in the other restaurant which was Tony's treat for my birthday.

Left Ventenac after refueling wine at the Chateau on **24th September** with Tony following us and picked up with another so we were three. Silly lock keeper at first lock (Ecluse Argens) with his interpretation of the new rules but his shop was doing a roaring trade. When we eventually left, we stopped for lunch, we passed two doubles (Penchlaurier and Ognon) and then the single at Homps, we continued but Jill & Tony stopped at Homps. We stopped at La Redorte and the Captain did the four-kilometre trek with the rucksack to do the shopping we then moved on into the countryside around PK134, lovely quiet mooring and good BBQ easier for Brandy.

The **25th September** turned out to be a lovely day, unknowingly passing the extra double lock (Puichéric) yesterday set us up for today. We virtually travelled alone in the locks due to the number going downstream. A very quick lunch at Trèbes, lock keeper started early and we gently sailed into Carcassonne and moored up at the Capitanerie at 17:00 hours for 15€. We found back the Vietnamese restaurant for supper, spoke to Jill & Tony who had a bad day and were at Trèbes for the night, what a difference a lock can make, we had done 18 today including two triples, one taking 20 minutes the other 25.

Left in a timely manner on **26th September** arriving at the first lock at 10:00 hours, there were three of us and it worked well with little or no waiting. Water level very bad and we were stuck for the third time on dropping the First Mate off at the landing point for Béteille, Captain finally got loose and then the third boat got stuck also and the lock keeper aided them with large pole. After that we decided to crawl along and eat a sandwich on the go, the other two stopped at Sauzens, we continued without further problems and moored up outside Guerre Lock (No. 28), beautiful spot and another good BBQ.

On the **27th September**, we had a later start waiting for Jill & Tony to avoid later problems with locks. In fact a couple of hold-ups for those going downstream, but we passed the four locks at St. Roch by 14:15, then gas oil and it seems to be using about two litres per hour on average, very good. So the usual return from Castelnaudary passing Laplanque, La Domergue, Laurens (triple), Du Roc (double) and finally the Mediterranean. One problem, filter or water pump? To be checked. The starboard bow prop stopped working at St. Roch and after the Captain swore in Ségala, it worked. We had an old deaf British guy with us in his little boat from Castelnaudary who 'helped'.

TOTAL TRIP: 543 Kilometres and 171 Locks not forgetting two swing bridges and crossing the Etang de Thau twice.

CHAPTER TEN – EVEN STRANGER TIMES

As I opened the logbook, I was shocked to find the next entries were for 2006! So much for our relaxed retirement, Sue started a Music Festival, which she ran for five years; although over a three-day period, it got bigger each year. It was run on the Esplanade in Ségala originally on a working pontoon loaned to us by VNF actually on the Canal du Midi, by the end we had to have another working stage on the Esplanade.

First Edition of FMSC at Ségala

It involved finding musicians organizing the programme and getting advertisements to cover the cost even though the Relais de Riquet 'fed and watered' the musicians. They basically played for the love of their music covering all genres from rap to opera. It was sad that no one took over when Sue decided she had to stop as by this time her Mother had come to live with us at the grand old age of 90 and stayed with us for five years until unfortunately we had to take her into care back in the UK. Also during this time frame, Jacques' Mum (Marraine) died whilst with us. Then one by one, our Labradors passed on to doggie heaven, Shandy, Whisky and our beloved boat companion Brandy.

Jacques had not been taking his retirement quietly either, feeling he had lost his written French (due to some thirty years of writing in English whilst working for NATO), he took on the job of local reporter for the Midi Libre, but guess who had to type up the reports: the old PA. In addition, there was the Age d'Or and helping at the Commune of Montferrand, so now it is easy to see the time slipping by again. The log book starts by saying that Deuxième Folie was in a clean and refurbished state, so that had been going on the background as I am sure we will have made some little trips to Castelnaudary, just for the pleasure.

It was **5th June 2006 – Pentecost** – when we set off with Véro & Bernard a boost for Véro's morale and a premiere for them both to be on the Canal having lived on the doorstep for many years. It is sad that they both have now passed having finally succumbed to the dreaded cancer. We locked with two others and after the slow start at Ecluse Mediterrean, it was plain sailing afterwards. We filled up with fuel (including a top up for the generator) at 11:15 hours and aimed for St. Roch, luck was with us and we were down the four locks in twenty minutes. We stopped for lunch with Véro and Bernard and then left them to find their way home and we were off on our own on the Canal with just one wait for one going upstream. Beautiful weather, both tired, having to get back into practice again, we moored up at Béteille at 18:30 hours, having covered thirty kilometres and twenty-seven locks and we actually gained a fender today rather than losing one. We were, however, suspecting a problem with the battery again; it always seems to be a problem for us.

So a lazy start on **6th June** around 10:30 hours, needed to use the generator so definitely a problem with the general battery. Another beautiful day and we had the canal to ourselves for most of the time. Stopped for the usual one hour for lunch at the double locks at Fresquel, where the lock keeper remembered us from helping Dominique by towing his 'wreck'. Continued to Trébes, busy as usual but only about one hour wait and we were the last ones down. What a sight at the bottom there was some twenty boats in line waiting to go up, they were in for a long wait. Such a lovely evening we continued cruising alone and finally moored up at Marseillette at 20:00 hours. Another one of our perennial problems the shower, it broke, to be mended in the morning. Only forty-one kilometres and thirteen locks that day.

Moved off on the **7th June** (after the First Mate had repaired the shower) with the continued beautiful weather around 10:15 hours thinking the 'pushers' had all passed. Not so, think we met the worst today several nationalities – dotty Spanish, the worst sort of Brits, nice Dutch. Did push at the end, one look at Homps was enough and we just made the last lock (Ecluse Argens) at 18:45 hours, and the lock keeper let us through, and we were now on the long stretch of fifty-four kilometres without locks. Captain lost a fender entering the last lock – rushing – Mate collected it. Definitely need a new battery; we moored up at Halte du Roubia.

The **8th June** was to be a 'slow boat to China' day, we made Ventenac and refueled the wine at the Chateau around 11:45 hours and then on to Le Somail (one of our favourite stops) moored for lunch and then a large Peniche passed at full speed tugging one of our picks out of the ground. Decided to move back nearer to the bridge and take the space the

Peniche had left, proper bollards and much safer mooring. First Mate managed to get the TV up and running and watched the ladies semi-finals and the Captain enjoyed the sun. We had our first meal out at the 'l'O à la Bouch' on the edge of the Canal du Midi – very good. Still battery problems so have to find a new one on the way.

A leisurely start on the **9th June** around 10:00 hours, it was change-over day for the hire boats and we had no fixed programme of where we might stop, Capestang was a possibility, but was full up of course as it was a hire boat base, including private moorings. Weather still nice but a little windy, stopped late for lunch at Poilhes and saw a ragondin (Coypu in English) and fed it some bread as it is an herbivore. Back in Ségala the locals have been known to eat them, we did not! We then moved on to Colombiers having passed the small Malpas tunnel, when the calm turned to storm with an objectionable 'Capitaine du Port', the incident happening around 16:00 hours, which resulted in us having to continue to the top of Foncérannes (Beziers) arriving around 17:30 hours having covered forty kilometres but no locks. Shower blew again and battery problem continues.

Early start on the **10th June** at 08:30 hours for the seven flight of locks at Foncérannes. One queue jumper (German) and then he fell in, smile time. We passed with four boats in total, Captain miscounted and thought there was one more and made a bad exit. All went well until the lock keeper squashed us in and we became hitched at Villeneuve les Beziers; there is a mention in the logbook here saying 'Hernia', the First Mate, pulled one, and was eventually operated on after our return home. First Mate did some running repairs and the Captain shopped. Had lunch and then moved on to the Portiragnes Lock where we made another mistake and got hitched on the other side – excellent lady lock keeper saved us. We then stopped at the Halte Nautique de Vias, free water, electricity and shop in the camping. We stayed an extra day here, ate chicken on the spit from the campsite, and generally relaxed after completing another twenty-one kilometres and thirty locks.

On the **12th June** we set off around 09:10 hours for Adge and its famous round lock, we lost one hour waiting for a phantom boat which never arrived. After that plain sailing, crossed the Etang de Thau using the GPS (no need of the fishermen this time), slightly bumpy but not too bad continuing to the Swing Bridge we were now again on the Canal du Rhone à Sete but hit mud. Therefore, no Peniche supper as we continued as far as the lock before the Marina at Lez at 18:45 – it was closed for the night! Whilst enroute and waiting for infamous bridge at Frontignan we had to move for a large waiting barge, after he had moored, we had to moor against him and await the 16:00 hours opening. Nothing going to plan today we arrived to spent the night at the Lez Pontoon and what we thought was not normal was NOT! the vannes had been left open by mistake or whatever.

Laurent and Eliane arrived at the pontoon on **13th June** and our suspicions of the night before were confirmed when we saw that the River Lez was dry. Catastrophic estimates varied from two to three days to seven to ten days for a refill. Dutch couple arrived in the morning who had planned to moor at the Marina and fly out of Montpellier, others who took their boat in too tired to move were stuck. Thanks to Laurent we got the new battery, the Mate installed it, and all back to normal again. However, it meant a change in plans, we moved eventually about 14:30 hours and found our mooring back in the countryside, Mate watched football, late super and then the ponies arrived, what a lovely sight, this had been Brandy's favourite mooring we wondered what she would have thought of them. We spent another night here relaxing, although the Captain did clean her windows, Mate did odd jobs and we cooked. Decision time and we decided to turn back in the morning.

The day of rest set us up nicely for a long day on the **15th June**, reaching the lifting bridge in time for 13:00 hours opening which turned out to be 13:30 hours. What a mess some people did make of it, not knowing the priority hence screaming French at a poor German on a small hire boat, without a book, did not help. Anyway, everyone got through then we crossed the Etang de Thau, the Mate using his GPS again, together with a catamaran who also must have had one and we were now back on the Canal du Midi. After we locked with him, he turned starboard after the Ecluse de Gard to go swimming in the Herault. We sailed on and through the round lock and reached the Vias moorings but had to use pickets as it was very busy, but we had a pizza from the campsite. The hose went again on the shower, needed a chandler but it broke again!

We took another day of rest on the **16th June** which passed quickly and then off we were on the **17th June**, it had rained overnight so much for the poor Captain's clean windows – well it was her fault she put 32 windows in Deuxième Folie. We had left about 10:00 hours so made the first lock and arrived at Villeneuve Les Beziers water and a petrol refill was done at Cassafières. Arrived at Ecluse 59 d'Ariège and it opened at 13:30 hours and we sailed in alone and then the at Ecluse 58 de Béziers the lock keep decided to open all vans Mate lost one rope and the Captain hung on for dear life, arm definitely better. At the next Ecluse l'Orb, we requested they go slower having told them our experience at the last one, then over the aqueduct and we were now enroute to join the queue for Foncérannes. Long wait, which was extended by a pleasure boat, which had priority, however, we had a fast rise as they opened three at a time. Moored around 18:15 hours around KM 204 (Ginestet) totally shattered (and only eleven locks and twenty-three kilometres – age is definitely catching up with us).

The **18th June** after an oil change we set off at 10:10 hours again a lovely day after a peaceful night in the countryside mooring we found. No locks so a gentle chugging along, Captain bumped into a bridge and lost a fender returned and recovered. No problems at the Malpas tunnel and we were now into our forty-three kilometre stretch without locks and arrived at Ventenac (where we moored for the night). Jacques and Brigitte joined us for drinks on board; we had of course refilled the red wine containers at the Chateau again! In the evening, we had supper out at Tony's old restaurant and tomorrow we start hitting the locks again.

Purchased bread etc. fed the ducks, no water available but had enough for a shower before we left on the **19th June** around 09:50 hours, smooth sailing, but as usual upstream locks are more tiring so Captain said enough at 15:00 hours just before next lock (Ecluse 52 Jouarres – PK143), nice mooring. Good decision watching all the shenanigans that went on, plus a pleasure boat. Again, we only managed six locks and eighteen kilometres!

The day dawned on the **20th June** and even with a 08:50 hours start it did not make much difference, although it was reasonable until lunch time and then it was never ending we were already too much into the season and too many boats which seem to get bigger every year so slower movement at the locks. We lost two more chunks of wood – one German and one Italian – too fast as usual. We waited two hours at the triple (Ecluse 48 Fonfile) and then arrived at Marseillette at 16:30 hours knackered, only sixteen kilometres covered and thirteen locks, not much considering the time it took and tomorrow we have Trèbes to look forward to.

Well the **21st June** turned into another one of those days with a boat problems, we had set off at 09:00 hours with the clock bonging the hour, peaceful trip to Trèbes and we left the triple at 12:00 hours good timing, excellent lock-keeper a really pleasurable rise. All continued well stopped in front of the next lock – 12:30 hours so lunch, waited at the next lock barely twenty minutes, and then on to the next triple Ecluse Fresquel which has a basin then followed by the following two. We made the basin got into the next one of the two and siren noises screamed from Deuxième Folie, no choice had to switch the engine off. Then pull ourselves into the third with the help of a German, then pull her out of that one this time with the help of two Australians, then we had to continue to pull her far enough into safety. The First Mate found the problem and had to change the pump and it took two hours, he was hot and dirty and we made one more lock (Ecluse St. Jean) at 18:45 and that got us into Carcassonne but not the Basin, just as well as it was 'Fête de la Musique'. New restaurant on the other side of the canal, which after showers we walked to – Excellent. Amusing incident with 'spooks' took us back to NATO times but this time we thought they might have been the Mafia.

22nd June we left making only one lock and two kilometres – the pump seized up in the lock, managed to cross the basin moored up with electricity and water. Looks like a serious problem a mechanic will arrive (hopefully) on 23rd June 09:00-10:00 hours, so we can foresee rescue service. He actually came on the 24th June listed all the problems and it was going to mean the boat had to stay for one week and Jill and Tony came to collect us.

We were told we had to leave AM Friday 30th June the latest! We were back on board on the 29th June, thanks again to Jill and Tony bringing us back to Carcassonne. Allan Marlow (the mechanic) arrived PM and after 45 minutes we were up and running, fantastic.

We were loaded up and ready to move by 1630 hours on the **29th June** and managed to pass four locks one with a passenger boat and hire boat, everything going smoothly engine hiccupped a little and then settled down we enjoyed the ride to Sauzens and found our wall for mooring with plenty of room. Still very hot and we picnicked under the shade of trees on the bank.

On **30th June,** we took an easy start at 09:30 hours and we were virtually on our own picked up one boat at Bram for two locks then stopped at Villepinte for lunch. We then moved off around 14:00 hours and we were alone for the rest of the trip all locks ready, always the same when you are not in a hurry. Stopped around 17:00 hours very tired we are beginning to think age is catching up on us for these trips. We had passed Bob on his fishing boat enroute for Scotland! We moored up at the back of a Routier, around PK68, where Michelle (Bonhomme – ex Relais de Riquet) now works, had an excellent steak. Captain in awkward mood, obviously over tired knocked over a litre jug of wine on a rug, which is now hanging over the canal, then a glass of wine on the new seats that washed off a dream, thank goodness.

The **1st July** saw us taking what would be our last trip back to Ségala, with a 09:00 hours, start the double was ready and we locked with one other, at St. Roch, we had to wait and then locked with the previous boat and a small British boat (young man) who had crossed over from Manchester. We then stopped to top up with fuel – 100 litres, continued passing the two singles before stopping for lunch. After lunch the triple, double and Mediterranean and sailed into Ségala still alone. Sylvie, Josianne and others came out to great us and we had a welcome beer. Tony took Jacques home for the car, the garage was at 35C and we ended up drinking water – believe it! however, that did not last long and we were back on the red wine.

TOTAL TRIP: 166 Locks, 458.5 Kilometres, 2 Tunnels and 2 Bridges.

EPILOGUE

This was always going to be the most difficult part to write, but I am sure it became evident in the last Chapter that age was catching up on us. With not only Deuxième Folie, leaping on and off and coping with locks but Troisème Folie also, large house, swimming pool, an acre of land going with it and the incumbent work it entailed. We could no longer cope and when you start paying, someone to do the jobs you used to do, it was decision time.

We put the house on the market, first sale fell through, but having cleaned up and emptied our beloved Deuxième Folie and put a for sale sign on her in 2007, then we had a buyer. A lovely young lady (Rose-Maryse Feuillert) who wanted to move it to Toulouse and use it as a houseboat and thus that is what happened. The Captain could not be there to see her being sailed away, tears are not far away now as I write this, but the First Mate did the job. Actually, Sue (no longer the Captain) was 'forced' to visit her in Toulouse and it was in fact a good thing, because it was not her boat anymore, the suite of furniture had gone from the living area; they actually cut it in half to get it out (sacrilege). The dining area was gone and it now contained a washing machine, this is just a couple of things to mention, she had changed, still had her name but she was not our Deuxième Folie anymore, but we often wonder if she is still there now.

The house finally sold during 2007, we moved to live on the Island of Madeira (Portugal) on 1st December, to continue our Folie's. That surprised everyone also, but it was the one place we had been on holiday to many times, which was unusual for us, as we liked to explore. We already had a parcel of land there (Quatrième Folie) but problems with building etc. and then we found a Penthouse and also bought the adjoining apartment knocking it all into one. The Follies were getting numerous at that point so having always kept the 'La Folie' sign we have reverted to that and still enjoying the sun and sea views, but feet are itching again!

Printed in the United States
By Bookmasters